Summary

Online Forex 8

Chapter 1 - Forex: the largest financial market in the world 13

   1.1 - How to enter the Forex 17

   1.2 - The main mechanisms that govern the Forex 21

   1.3 - The Pareto principle 25

   1.4 – What are currencies 30

      1.4.1 – Cross majors 31

      1.4.2 – Cross Minors 37

      1.4.3 – Exotic currency pairs 39

      1.4.4 – Cryptocurrencies 41

   1.5 – Observe the spread and the pip to get profits 44

   1.6 – Forex trading today 47

Chapter 2 - How to make money in Forex 52

  2.1 – Implementation of a valid strategy 55

    2.1.1 – Money Management....................57

    2.1.2 – Risk Management 62

  2.2 – Trend analysis 68

    2.2.1 – Technical Analysis 70

    2.2.2. – Fundamental Analysis 78

  2.3 – The study of volatility and market expectations..84

  2.4 – Signal reception....................................89

Chapter 3 – Brokers 92

  3.1 – Who are the brokers? 93

  3.2 – What role do brokers play in Forex?....94

  3.3 – How to invest with brokers 96

    3.3.1 – CFD 98

    3.3.2 – Binary options 99

    3.3.3 – Forex 100

- 3.3.4 – Social Trading 101
- 3.3 – Trading platforms.............................103
- Fundamental Analysis 105
- Chapter 1 - What is Fundamental Analysis 108
  - 1.1 – Main differences between Fundamental Analysis and Technical Analysis 116
  - 1.2 – What is the Fundamental Analysis for? 125
  - 1.3 – Data collection and analysis..............134
    - 1.3.1 – Macroeconomic data 139
    - 1.3.2 – Microeconomics data..................146
  - 1.4 – Operational difficulties in applying the Fundamental Analysis 150
- Chapter 2 - The financial statements and the Fundamental Analysis 156
  - 2.1 – Budget structure 160
    - 2.1.1 – Balance Sheet.............................162
    - 2.1.2 – Income Statement......................165

2.1.3 – Notes to the financial statements and cash flow statement.........................169

2.2 – Analysis of the financial statement indicators useful for Fundamental Analysis 175

2.2.1 - Earning Before Interest, Taxes, Depreciation and Amortization...............176

2.2.2 – Return On Equity........................179

2.2.3 – Return On Investment................181

Chapter 3 - Fundamental Analysis in the stock market and Forex...183

3.1 – The stock market: sector analysis and company valuation 187

3.2 – The intrinsic value of equities 191

3.2.2 – The market multiples method....198

3.3 – The real estate sector 202

3.4 – Fundamental Analysis in Forex 211

3.4.1 – The Monetary Policy of the Central Banks...217

- 3.4.2 – The economy 218
- 3.4.3 – The trend in gold and oil commodities 220

Conclusions 223

Operating Forex Trading 226

Chapter 1 - What is Forex Trading 230
- 1.1 – How Forex is born 232
- 1.2 – The main advantages 241
- 1.3 – The subjects in the Forex market 247
- 1.4 – Capital management 256
- 1.5 – Forex Trading Indices 264
- 1.6 – The times at which to trade 269
  - 1.6.1 – Forex in America 271
  - 1.6.2 – Forex in Europa 273
  - 1.6.3 – Forex in Asia 275
- 2.1 – Stop-loss 279
- 2.2 – Take Profit 284

2.3 – Market orders 289

2.4 – Limit orders 292

Chapter 3 - Fundamental Analysis and Technical Analysis 296

   3.1 – Fundamental Analysis: macroeconomic indicators 302

   3.2 – The three pillars of Technical Analysis 307

   3.3 – Dow's Theory 311

   3.4 – The Momentum and Fibonacci retracements 320

   3.5 – Overbought and oversold 326

   4.1 – The moving averages 330

   4.3 – Relative Strenght Index 334

   4.4 – Adverage Directional Index 336

   4.5 – The stochastic oscillator 338

Conclusions 341

Online Forex

The Forex market can be imagined from two different points of view. The first image is certainly positive, that is the vision of a financial market that is able to offer anyone the possibility of easily making profits: an opportunity to round up one's salary or even to transform investment into a real work. The second image is negative. The Forex can indeed be seen as a money-eating system, illusory and bankrupt.

In reality, both visions are wrong. In fact, Forex is a system that allows for gains in the medium-long term, but only for those who decide to implement a strategy correctly, dedicating both money and time to the market. In fact, trading is complicated and difficult, but not random activity. This concept is very important as it means that any fluctuation could be anticipated correctly by investors. However, there are a number of theories and tools that can simplify their tasks. But even these tools require time and money to function properly and send the right signals to the trader.

The brokers, with the advent of the internet, have made different platforms available to their users. They have some fundamental indicators and oscillators and translate the oscillatory movements of the market on the charts, so as to simplify their reading.

However, it is necessary to always consider the risks associated with the trading activity. In fact, investments in the financial market offer as many profits as losses. It is impossible to eliminate the negative components, which may be due to incorrect strategies, lateral phases of the market and normal competition present in Forex. The losses, therefore, must be received according to a positive vision, accepting them as much as the profits. It is true that there are few traders who succeed in making profits in the long run, but it is also true that few investors enter the market in a rational manner, without being carried away by revenge or by the will to carry out simple attempts to become rich.

Once the strategy has been implemented, in fact, it is necessary to follow it assiduously, unless it presents some gaps and requires instrumental corrections.

The concept is to "play" responsibly, that is to invest one's capital with the knowledge that success and failure rates can be almost similar. In fact, the first objective must be to develop a strategy capable of minimizing the risks of the trader.

Chapter 1 - Forex: the largest financial market in the world

Forex is considered the largest financial market in the world. This statement is confirmed by the enormous amount of trade volumes that are exchanged daily within it. Forex is also the only market in the world to remain open uninterruptedly for five days a week, allowing traders to make their investments at any time of day or night.

The term Forex is derived from the union of two words, namely Foreign and Exchange, which allow it to be identified as the foreign currency market. Precisely for this reason, it is easy to imagine Forex as the most frenetic market on the entire planet, which at the same time allows traders who decide to invest in it to make greater gains.

To be able to make the trading activity advantageous, however, it is necessary to devote time and money to study Forex and the currencies traded in it, but also to engage in order to implement an investment strategy that allows profits to be made in the medium and long term.

Naturally, as an investment activity, every trader has to study and contemplate the percentage of risk. No strategy, not even that considered almost perfect will be able to guarantee the complete elimination of losses, which however will have to be reduced in such a way as to optimize the relationship between yield and risk. To think of relying totally on chance, on the other hand, is the worst idea an investor who wants to be successful can have.

The fluctuations, albeit minimal and centesimal, relative to the currency trading carried out in the Forex, are not in fact given by chance but are the result of a series of mechanisms and events that the trader must be able to understand. A profit will be made when a trader succeeds in correctly anticipating a future oscillation. Naturally, this profit will increase proportionally to the percentage of risk present in the operation carried out.

It is obvious that each trader will have to implement a strategy based on the objectives he or she aims to achieve. People have different risk appetite and this feature also affects the world of trading.

But there are so many other differences that distinguish one trader from another. For example, in the financial market, investments can be made in a very short time, even within a day, or in a very long time: the choice of the type of trading to opt for will depend on the balance that the trader will be able to give to the relationship between rationality and will to make profits as fast as possible.

1.1 - How to enter the Forex

Getting into Forex today is very simple, but it hasn't always been that way. Until the 1990s, investors who intended to open a specific transaction on the market were forced to physically go to financial agencies or to specific licensed banks. Only after a long wait, due to the countless number of investors, and confusion, could he open his transaction. But even this process did not take place in a timely manner and so opportunities often disappeared and a probable profit soon became a certain loss.

The internet has profoundly changed not only the Forex but also the financial markets. Today, in fact, investing in the Forex market is very simple and it takes just a few moments and a single click to do so. Investments can be made from anywhere: the only requirements are a device with web access and a sufficiently stable internet connection.

Another difference is the costs of entering the market. In fact, every single transaction carried out in the past by an investor was accompanied by very high commission costs. This made trading an exclusive activity for a few subjects, that is, only for those with an initial capital large enough to be able to sustain negative phases of the market that could last for a long time. Today, on the other hand, brokers have decided to cancel commission costs. This decision has an important consequence, as it allows everyone, even those with little or no experience in the world of trading, to access Forex, regardless of thecapital held.

The brokers have therefore attracted an enormous number of subjects, sometimes boasting easy profits, with the aim of increasing market volumes. At the same time, the total opening up of financial markets has given the opportunity even to inexperienced subjects, after periods of study, analysis and experience, to become professional traders.

1.2 - The main mechanisms that govern the Forex

The Forex market is governed by mechanisms that are simple enough to understand, as it is focused on currency trading. This does not mean, however, that trading is easy.

Simplicity lies in the fact that, unlike the stock market and the commodity market, Forex excludes the presence of companies. The value of currencies, that is of the elements of exchange in Forex, is mainly influenced by central banks, which through the implementation of certain monetary policies, influences interest rates and, consequently, the nominal value of money. Therefore, in order to be efficient within Forex, traders will always need to be informed about all the economic and financial events that may affect the Forex market and the items traded in it. As a currency market, it is subject to real fluctuations rather than to trends, which concern stocks and indices.

This difference derives from the fact that, while the indices depend on the willingness of the individual companies to earn, the currencies are tools that represent the economy, and in particular the import and export data of a single nation, and for this reason, they tend more floating in the market. This is to be considered a very favorable characteristic for traders, as it makes Forex much more predictable than all other financial markets.

If the mechanisms of Forex are too complicated to understand and analyze, then it is possible to rely on some tricks that allow you to copy the strategies implemented by professional traders. These techniques, known as Copytrading, can be adapted on the basis of the capital held, allocating only a low percentage of the same for each individual transaction and increasing the investments only if the ratio between yield and risk is sufficiently high.

1.3 - The Pareto principle

The Pareto principle is one of the laws that govern the entire universe. It is a non-physical law, as it has no certain thesis that identifies it, but at the same time, it appears very valid. It is possible to speak of a sort of golden relationship between contrasting elements, in a complete antithesis between them. One of the two elements, in fact, will be numerically or volumetrically larger or wider than the other, in a ratio that is around 80% against 20%.

This principle, as mentioned, regulates the entire universe and, consequently, also the financial markets and specifically the Forex market. Many traders can avoid or disregard this principle, but in reality, it has been statistically stated that about 80% of traders investing in Forex lose the allocated capital. Of course, this data also includes traders who have never studied the basics of trading, nor even analyzed the market. Therefore, going deeper into the mechanisms that govern the Forex would allow traders to move away from 80% Pareto. Nevertheless, it is still statistically confirmed that only 20% of investors manage to pursue a strategy that allows them to constantly make profits.

The Paretian principle applies especially to human psychology and this also applies to the world of trading. The approach to the market and the psychological aspect of the traders are indeed fundamental to understand if the road taken will lead to success or failure. The strategies often fail because the investors do not follow them assiduously, letting themselves be carried away by temptations and not acting on the market with rationality.

The openings of the positions are also regulated by the absolute principle of Pareto. In fact, it is statistically proven that in a well-defined time interval, 80% of it does not allow safe entry into the market, while in the remaining 20%, it is possible to make profitable transactions. Also, in this case, the psychological errors detectable in the haste to open a position or in an attempt to redeem immediately from a negative operation, are to be considered the main elements that lead to failure.

As long as a human remains the architect of his or her own investment, psychological errors will always be protagonists of the financial markets, and the Pareto concept will always have reason to be valid.

1.4 – What are currencies

The currency is considered the object of the Forex market and is considered as the unit of exchange through which it is possible to exchange goods and services. The currency can take both the form of money and be completely virtual. The currency is generally issued by the national central bank.

In Forex, the sale takes place between two different currencies: the currency is the currency of the country. In currency pairs, the first monetary symbol shown represents the base currency, while the second symbol is considered the quote currency. The value of the couple, however, is unique and does not refer to the individual curriculum indicated, but to their relationship. If this value exceeds 1.0, then the first of the two currencies is stronger than the second, vice versa if the value is less than 1.0, then the second currency will be considered the stronger one in the ratio.

1.4.1 – Cross majors

Major or cross major currencies are the most traded currency pairs worldwide, considering the generality of financial markets. They are mainly four and the US dollar is considered as the absolute protagonist, which is, in fact, part of all major pairs.

The main Major is the EUR / USD, or Euro-US Dollar, as these two currencies are the currencies traded in the geographic areas considered to be the most important economies in the world, namely Europe and the United States respectively. Not to be overlooked, this pair also represents the younger cross major, as the European currency has only entered circulation since 2002. Being the main currency pair traded on the market, the EUR / USD shows a very high volatility rate, which translates into reduced spread values. Therefore, traders will find the offers relating to the sale or purchase of these cross majors very easily. The volatility rate is however established both by the ECB, that is, the European Central Bank, and by the FED, or the Federal Reserve, which alter the strength of the controlled currency by increasing or decreasing interest rates.

The USD / JPY, or US Dollar-Japanese Yen, is the second most important Major Pair. Traders take advantage of the difference in value between the two currencies to invest in what is alled carry trading, which is an operation that requires a loan in a country that uses a currency with very low interest rates and then uses the money received to invest in countries with high interest rates. The Japanese Central Bank, or Bank of Japan, has in fact fought low inflation for many years, considerably reducing interest rates, sometimes even wiping them out. Also, for this reason, the JPY is seen as a safe haven, as it shows a positive trend at times when the economy is going through negative phases. Operations of this kind are however complicated and, in order to achieve the set objectives, require a remarkable experience.

Among the cross majors, there was absolutely no lack of the currency pair GBP

/ USD, meaning the British pound-US dollar, known to all traders with the term cable, or the ocean cable used for so many years to communicate the exchange rate between these two currencies. The Pound was the reference currency of all financial markets for many years before the US dollar took its place. The Pound, despite the fact that the United Kingdom has never actually been part of the European Union, links its value and its financial performance to the European economy. Therefore, the volumes included in this cross major can be considered similar to those of the EUR / USD pair. In addition to the Federal

Reserve, the protagonist of this pair is the Bank of England, which modifies the value of its currency on the basis of the monetary policy undertaken.

The last major pair is made up of the US dollar and the Swiss franc, therefore USD / CHF. The Swiss franc is also one the major currencies because it is considered a safe haven. In addition, the stability and perennial neutrality of Switzerland guarantee traders a fairly linear fluctuation in values. Moreover, when the market has relatively low volatility rates, the Swiss franc, due to its geographical position, tends to follow the trend of the Euro.

1.4.2 – Cross Minors

There are a number of currency reports that are not linked to the US dollar, and which are considered to be of lesser importance than the former, and for this reason they are defined as cross-minor. However, these relationships must not be underestimated by traders, either because they influence the major somehow, or because they represent a large part of the Forex volumes. Thus, investors can reap many benefits by investing in the performance of these currency pairs.

The minor crosses relate to the various relationships between the Euro, the Japanese Yen, the British Pound, the Swiss Franc, the Canadian Dollar, the Australian Dollar and the New Zealand Dollar.

To obtain the exchange rates of each minor currency report in the past, it was necessary to convert the base currency into US dollar and then convert it into the quote currency. Today, thanks to the presence of these secondary intersections, the trader is no longer required to carry out this operation and the investments will be faster and more direct.

1.4.3 – Exotic currency pairs

The relationship between one of the four cross major currencies with a currency of economically young or small nations gives birth to an exotic currency pair. Of course, this kind of currencies is traded less frequently on financial markets and within Forex, and for this reason, the commission costs related to individual transactions are generally higher than those related to other currency pairs.

Among the currencies of emerging or smaller countries of note, those of two very important Asian countries stand out, namely Singapore and Hong Kong, but also currencies of countries belonging to the European continent not included in the Eurozone, such as the Turkish Lira and the crowns of the Nordic and Scandinavian countries. Finally, a currency that is becoming increasingly important in the financial market is represented by the South African Rand, which is also included in exotic currency pairs.

1.4.4 – Cryptocurrencies

Cryptocurrencies can be considered as digital currencies without any control by supervisory bodies, and for this reason, it is decentralized. Just the lack of real control has allowed this type of currency to spread easily around the world and to be traded within the financial markets. The main feature of cryptocurrencies is the presence of a very high volatility rate.

The trader will naturally have to foresee the possible evolution of the cryptocurrency observed in the market, trying to buy at relatively low values and then selling at high values. Moreover, even in this market, it is possible to invest by anticipating any future declines in cryptocurrencies, thus selling out in the open.

The best-known cryptocurrency in the world is certainly Bitcoin, which was born in Japan in 2009. Bitcoin was the first cryptocurrency to be accepted as a form of payment on the web. Of course, being totally based on cryptography and on a centralized payment system, known as Proof of Work, Bitcoin has managed to break free from traditional banking circuits, while still guaranteeing the same level of security in digital money exchanges.

To date, cryptocurrencies are therefore used both to buy certain goods or services and to transfer or receive monetary values.

1.5 – Observe the spread and the pip to get profits

Trading in Forex and in all other markets is carried out by considering two essential elements. The first is certainly the price at which a given transaction is sold, and this value is referred to as Bid. The second element is the purchase price of the same operation and it is referred to in a technical jargon as Ask.

The difference between the two elements, namely between Bid and Ask, gives the trader the value of the spread. This difference is nothing more than the commission that each broker receives as gain for every single transaction opened on the market. The calculation of the spread is fundamental for a trader as it helps to identify which transactions are really advantageous, based on the forecasts made and the strategy that the investor has decided to adopt.

Another fundamental element is the percentage of point, also known with the acronym pip. The pip represents the basic unit of the entire Forex, as it indicates the smallest possible fluctuation for a currency pair. Calculating the percentage of point is very simple. It is, in fact, represented by the difference between the fourth decimal digit of the values of a currency pair observed at two different time points.

Since the pip is the unit of measurement of fluctuations within Forex, it is natural that the spread is also expressed in terms of pips. The value of the spread is in any case decided by the broker to whom the trader has decided to rely on. Each investor is therefore required to evaluate the convenience of opening the same transaction with different brokers.

1.6 – Forex trading today

The trading activity has undergone profound changes over the years. The most important of these transformations has certainly occurred with the advent of the web that has practically liberalized the Forex, making it accessible to all.

Today, Forex is considered the safest financial market in the world, as risks are minimized and returns are optimized.

The main advantage of modern online trading is the elimination of commission costs. The brokers, in fact, now make gains only from the spreads calculated on the currency pairs traded in the Forex.

Furthermore, today's Forex allows you to trade at any time of day or night, taking advantage of market openings and closures, depending on their business hours.

Modern trading allows profits to be made despite very low investments. This is possible thanks to the effect of financial leverage, which makes it possible to amplify the investment made even by 300 or 400 times. The higher the possibility of increasing any profit, the greater the risk associated with the transaction. Therefore, it is up to the trader to define and implement his or her own strategy, contemplating all these elements, choosing the most profitable hours and deciding the amount of optimal capital to be allocated for each market segment.

But what most distinguishes modern trading is the fundamental need to understand the market in all its aspects in order to correctly anticipate currency fluctuations. Imagining Forex as a random market is completely wrong. The fluctuations, according to the most important technical analysis theories, are indeed predictable, and there are a number of tools that facilitate the identification of trends and possible future values.

In particular, modern Forex requires the alienation of the emotional component from the investment activity. In fact, humans are excessively exposed to stress and tension, and sometimes open positions on the market driven more by the desire for revenge against a loss just suffered than by rationality. In this sense, we risk sending an entire strategy, even well-designed, into the air with investments that are completely entrusted to chance. This attitude does not characterize successful traders, who follow what they had previously implemented to the letter, accepting losses and waiting patiently for the right time to make the investment.

Chapter 2 - How to make money in Forex

The gain in the world of Forex is a concept linked to both risk and the management of available capital. It is precisely for this reason that it is important to diversify the strategy implemented on several matrices, following different ways to achieve the same goal, namely profit.

Therefore, there is no easy gain even in Forex. In fact, success is the result of a long and tortuous path, which will put traders in difficulty and require time, even a lot of money. So investors will have to find a method of action that minimizes the risk but does not make the yield drop too much. The balance in the relationship between these two factors is to be found in one's own nature. Each person has a different risk appetite than the other, and this is reflected in different strategies in the Forex world.

But trading also requires passion, perseverance, and commitment. Only through these three virtues will a trader engage in the study of fundamental and theoretical concepts, in the analysis of the market and in the implementation of a strategy that can lead to success.

Furthermore, each trader will have to put his or her illusions on one side. In fact, the Forex is a unique world, which offers possibilities that very few other realities are able to grant. However, it is necessary to set goals that are realistic and above all achievable. For inexperienced and novice traders, it is advisable to entrust their investments to a demo account, that is an account that allows the use of fictitious virtual money to carry out Forex trading.

2.1 – Implementation of a valid strategy

So the first real step that every trader must take, after having studied all the mechanisms that regulate the market, is to implement a real strategy that allows him or her to stay in Forex in the long term.

There is no real strategic model that can be considered better than another, but above all, there is no perfect strategy that can completely avoid losses. Of course, there are fundamental concepts that during the implementation phase the trader must try to respect, so as to increase the probability of success. Many experts compare the importance for the trader to create his or her own strategy that adapts to his or her style and goals, to the importance of generating an excellent business plan for companies that intend to establish themselves in the competitive market.

Therefore, the strategy of each trader must focus on two concepts: Money Management, i.e. the management of capital, and Risk Management.

2.1.1 – Money Management

Capital management, known in technical jargon as Money Management, refers to all the operations through which a trader can invest and at the same time protect his or her own capital.

First of all, the trader will have to understand the amount of capital to be allocated for each individual investment. In fact, a strategy consists of more investments, sometimes even contemporary ones, which may be carried out based on different approaches and trading methods. This choice is certainly personal, as it is closely linked to both the investor's risk appetite and the amount of capital he or she has.

Furthermore, a strategy must be implemented in such a way that it can protect the invested capital. Once a trader has opened a certain position, it is necessary to monitor currency fluctuations following a very specific concept: he or she is required to stop losses and let profits run. Therefore, the trader has to identify what are the possible points of exit from the market: letting go of losses in the hope that there is a sudden fluctuation that brings the currency pair back to a position advantageous for him or her is very risky and therefore counterproductive; but letting profits go too far can be harmful, as doing so increases the level of risk more and more, and a sudden price fluctuation could generate a loss. Therefore, the trader must behave in a rational way, and never follow the avarice. Every profit must be seen as a positive operation and never as a missed opportunity.

Even if all these operations, related to the opening and closing of a position within Forex, are delegated by the trader to an automated trading system, the concept just expressed must not be altered. Establishing a correct strategy to define the right time to exit the market is probably more important than achieving excellent entry strategies. In fact, it is precisely in the closure that it is possible to optimize profits or minimize losses.

To be able to monitor all these conditions at the same time, but also to be able to foresee possible future scenarios that could influence, for better or for worse, the open position, the trader can rely on some tools that can generate very useful signals. These signals induce the investor, or the Trading System, to open positions, close them and even reopen them, although the exit from the market has already occurred, in the event that certain conditions are met.

Therefore, Money Management is an element of the strategy that embraces all the phases of trading, from the analysis of the market to the closing of the open positions in it. Many experts consider the management of capital as the fundamental part of the entire currency investment and the causes of possible failure and merits for the possible generation of profits are also attributed it.

2.1.2 – Risk Management

The second element that allows a trader to take the road to success is that relating to risk management, that is, Risk Management. Naturally, the implementation of this process focuses mainly on identifying risky events or strategic components that can generate unwanted risks.

Risk management consists mainly of three modes of action. The first refers to the possibility of transferring risk to third parties, competitors on the market; the second involves the attempt to completely avoid the risk; the third method, finally, involves the acceptance of risk, with the consequent attempt to limit and minimize the negative components.

What the trader must absolutely avoid is the achievement, following a series of losses, of a financial risk, which would entail the total loss of the capital initially allocated in the trading activity.

Once the risks have been identified, the trader is required to analyze them, in order to understand what their actual level of danger is. Therefore, risk assessment allows a strategy to be drawn up which is able to avoid or limit the most urgent risky events, leaving aside those considered less dangerous, at least temporarily. But to get an accurate analysis, the trader should study the actual causes that lead to the generation of the risk and, above all, the consequences that this risk entails. This is certainly the most delicate phase of the entire Risk Management. If you know both the causes and the consequences of a risk, then you can consider yourself able to modify the strategy in an optimal way, in order to minimize the negative results. But this is not always possible within Forex, because of the speed with which the market evolves, and because of the lack of suitable elements to understand the origins and effects of the risk.

Careful evaluation naturally leads to the definition of priorities. The implemented strategy must be able to react promptly to risks, but following both a chronological and economic order. In fact, based on the assessments done on individual risks, the trader will have to decide how much capital to allocate.

This suggests the intense correlation that links Money Management with Risk Management. Both processes are decisive for the implementation of a strategy capable of reacting to internal and external market events, both promptly and with rationality. The task of the trader, therefore, appears very complicated, but even in this case, there are tools that allow to simplify and, above all, to speed up his or her work.

It is therefore very important that every investor, in addition to knowing how to correctly interpret the market, tends to improve in the use of these tools, in such a way as to greatly facilitate its function, delegating to software and automated

systems the tasks that it would have had to perform first person.

2.2 – Trend analysis

Once the trader has analyzed all the internal and external market factors, studied the economic events that could somehow influence the value of the currency pairs and implemented a hypothetically valid strategy, then he or she can move on to analyze the trend or the fluctuations that characterize the Forex.

Many of the analysts of the past have shown that the evolution of the trends is not absolutely accidental, but preventable by examining the historical series, the economic calendar and other social and political events that could influence the financial markets. However, the trend analysis follows two different theoretical directions. The first, based on the assiduous study of the market and trends, is called Technical Analysis; the second, which focuses attention on the events marked on the economic calendar, is called Fundamental Analysis.

2.2.1 – Technical Analysis

The Technical Analysis involves the use of graphs and indicators in order to identify the possible evolution of the currency market. This method of analysis is based on theories of traders and analysts who have over the years succeeded in upsetting the financial market, and making profits in the darkest moments of world economic history.

The main purpose of the Technical Analysis consists of identifying a possible inversion in the trend of a trend. Therefore, the idea is to follow the trend of a trend until it reaches a resistance or support, thus ending up in an overbought or oversold area. At this point, the chances of incurring a turnaround increase and the trader tries to make a profit from the situation that has arisen.

But to understand the actual trend of the trend, the technical analyst must necessarily be based on three fundamental principles. The first states that prices discount everything. This means that, at least theoretically, the trader is not required to study in-depth all the events and factors that can influence a trend, as these conditions are already inherent within the trend. For this reason, it is only necessary to analyze the trend. This is completed with all the information necessary to be able to act correctly on the financial market. The second assumption refers to human behavior. According to the theory of technical analysis, traders tend not to control their emotions, having a euphoric behavior when prices follow a trend and panicking once the trend seems to have exhausted its strength. For this reason, every trend will follow an oscillatory trend, upward and downward, precisely dictated by the behavior of investors. In this sense, it is possible for the technical analyst to identify the possible future evolution of the trend based on his or her past performance. This means that for the Technical Analysis, history repeats itself and it becomes fundamental to analyze the historical series of each trend to obtain advantages in terms of gain by investing in them. The third fundamental assumption of Technical Analysis involves the concept of validity of the trend. In fact, a trend is considered valid until the trader observes clear signs that indicate a reversal. Therefore, a small downward price correction on an uptrend cannot be exchanged for a reversal, which means that the trend has remained valid. This assumption is especially followed by 'trend following,' that is a kind of investors who stubbornly pursue the trend until the actual reversal occurs.

Dow Theory is considered the pinnacle of the entire Technical Analysis. Dow founded his market analysis on six fundamental points, reported in the articles of the Wall Street Journal. The first point of Dow's theory coincides with the first assumption of Technical Analysis, that is, prices discount everything. In the second point of Dow's Theory, a trend is divided according to its gender: primary trend, when it has a duration of more than one year; secondary trend, which can last from three weeks to three months; a minor trend that has a duration of less than three weeks. In the third point, Dow divides the primary trend into three components, depending on the maturation achieved: the accumulation phase, during which the trend is born; the consolidation phase, during which investors identify the new trend and open positions on the market; the third phase, during which the trend loses intensity and the traders close the previously open positions in order to make profits from the price spread. The fourth point of Dow's Theory refers to the fact that if two indices move in the same direction, then the observed trend is still valid. Further confirmation of the validity of the trend must arrive, according to the fifth point of Dow's Theory, from market volumes, which expand or decrease depending on its intensity. Finally, the sixth point indicates the proximity of the trend towards the trader, almost as a sign of friendship. Therefore, the investor must trust the trend until the moment he or she clearly and definitively reverses his or her performance.

The Dow Theory, despite having been written at the beginning of the 20th century, still appears valid and effective. Therefore, the technical analyst is bound to faithfully follow these concepts or to impose them on an automated trading system, in order to succeed in Forex.

In addition to these theoretical concepts, the technical analyst bases his or her investments on certain instruments, such as graphs, indicators and oscillators. Through these, the trader will be able to better understand the market, will perceive the trend of currency pairs and will be able to anticipate future developments.

2.2.2. – Fundamental Analysis

If the technical analyst bases his or her action on the in-depth study of the markets and its historical series, the fundamental analyst focuses more on all those events that can cause fluctuations in trends within Forex. These events can be both budgeted, such as the publication of a balance sheet of an important company active in the financial market of interest, or sudden events, such as the collapse of a political government. The effects of these events can be manifold and the fundamental analyst must be able to understand whether the trends will turn up or down, depending on the currency pair observed.

All relevant economic events must be included in a calendar, which must be regularly consulted by the trader. Future investment strategies will be based on it.

The main element of interest for a fundamental analyst is certainly the financial statements of a company or a major body within Forex. However, to be able to anticipate the trend, the analyst will have to research and study the unofficial balance sheet, generally announced a few days earlier than the actual one. The financial statements, and in particular EBITDA, ROE and ROI must be applied to it in order to understand the state of health of the analyzed company.

The EBITDA is the partial result of the reclassified income statement, which takes into consideration the income deriving solely from the operating management. Therefore, it is the value of income before interest, depreciation, amortization and taxes are added to it algebraically. It indicates the real state of the company, seen not in a particular moment, but in an interval of time. The elements of the Income Statement are flow values, that is in continuous evolution, and not stocks, such as those present in the Balance Sheet. The ROE index, an acronym for Return on Equity, considers the relationship between the net income of the company and its own capital. In this way, the trader is able to understand how much of his or her own financial means used by the company turns into income: the greater this percentage, the better the state of health of the company. Finally, the ROI makes it possible to understand how much of the capital invested has actually turned into income. It is a simple index to apply, but which must be interpreted correctly by the trader to bring about advantages in trading.

The role of the two analysts is in some ways opposite. The technical analyst is obliged to engage in the phase prior to the investment, with an in-depth study of all the historical series, the factors surrounding the Forex environment and with constant monitoring of open positions in the market. Vice versa, the fundamental analyst focuses his or her efforts on the days preceding a specific economic event that can influence the fluctuations of currency pairs, hypothesizing all possible future scenarios based on the economic-financial data of one or more companies and the results obtained by applying the financial statement ratios.

It is impossible to state a priori which of the two methodologies of approach to the market is more advantageous. In fact, each technique has strengths and weaknesses, and each one is better suited to specific market phases. Professional traders carry out several strategies, some based on Technical Analysis and others on Fundamental Analysis, in such a way as to be able to exploit the strengths of both methodologies and cover each other's weaknesses.

2.3 – The study of volatility and market expectations

Volatility is an important indicator of the stability, and consequently of the instability, of a market. It can be calculated on a daily basis or on a periodic basis and allows to know what the actual strength of a trend is, its intensity and, indirectly, its duration. It is possible to consider two different types of volatility, historical and implicit.

Traders use historical volatility to understand what market reactions may be following certain events. They consider the periods characterized by a high or low volatility rate and analyze the responses of the currency pairs to the events marked in the economic calendar. The concept is that the same couple will react similarly to events of a similar nature, and following this idea, it will be more likely to detect future fluctuations in Forex. This type of calculation is best suited to the fundamental analyst.

The implied volatility, on the other hand, is intended to identify the future volatility relating to a specific currency pair. To obtain this indication, the trader is required to compare the curve of demand and supply and all the factors that can influence the trends of these lines. It is a job much more suitable for the technical analyst.

There are numerous tools that can capture and accurately indicate the volatility rate on the market. These tools can be combined together to obtain more precise data and information, optimizing the trader's strategy. In addition to the present and future volatility rate, the charts, indicators and oscillators allow us to obtain important information regarding market expectations. It is possible to find more or less valid information on the web about the future trend of the market, but every investor should research his or her information using his or her own tools, in order to purify the statistics and data obtained from any other influence.

Every active subject has market expectations. If a subject has considerable importance in Forex, then his or her expectation may also influence those of the other subjects. If the general expectation is almost identical, then the trend could really follow that trend, unless there are extraordinary events that alter the market. However, it remains difficult to have a unanimous idea of the market, especially when the strength of buyers and sellers is equivalent.

2.4 – Signal reception

Market expectations can be intuited especially by combining the action of tools and software that allow the market to be analyzed.

Charts are the first tools used by traders. These can be inversion, when they are intended to sense a possible reversal of trend orientation or continuation. The figures that the trends create allow traders to understand what the next evolution of the trend may be, opening and closing positions depending on the time of the market.

The second type of instruments are the oscillators, which draw a hypothetical trend that fluctuates within a range, depending on the values assumed by the market. The oscillators are fundamental to understand if the values of the currency pairs have entered into areas of oversold or overbought so that the trader can invest by acting accordingly.

Finally, the indicators make it possible to follow the market trend. These instruments, unlike oscillators, do not allow to identify areas of inversion, but rather allow the trader to decipher the intensity and strength of the trend, in such a way as to leave his or her position open by exploiting each step. The trend is pursued until it shows an obvious signal of trend variation.

Each tool is very useful for the trader, but to fully exploit its potential, it is necessary to combine their actions. It is only possible in this way to fill some gaps and increase the chances of making profits in the medium-long term.

Chapter 3 – Brokers

In the financial sector and especially in the trading sector, the broker plays a fundamental role, representing the most significant profession in the finance and securities market. The broker market is vast, and each of them offers customers different and personalized services, based on needs. However, brokers do not represent a foolproof system to earn money, as they must always be used without losing sight of the right level of risk beyond which it would be better not to go.

3.1 – Who are the brokers?

Financial brokers are professionals who act as intermediaries between investors and the financial market. In reality, intermediaries that operate in other markets other than financial markets can also be called brokers, such as insurance brokers, shipbrokers, and aeronautical brokers.

The significant figure in the world of trading and investments, however, is that of the financial broker, who today also performs the function of a market maker, that is, deals with the management of the market.

3.2 – What role do brokers play in Forex?

The broker does not only play the role of financial intermediary. In fact, from the legislative point of view, the broker is obliged to protect the investor, informing and covering him or her against risks, but also carrying out assistance duties, both in the phase prior to the investment, and to that strictly inherent to the same.

Over the years, with the transformation of the financial market, the role of the broker has also changed. Initially, the intermediaries made gains especially from the commissions, which until a few decades ago turned out to be very high. Nowadays, the brokers, also covering a task of protecting investors, have reduced or even zeroed the cost related to the commissions for opening transactions in the Forex. Their profits today are generated with spreads, that is with the price difference between two values of the same currency pair observed in two different periods.

So the brokers work alongside the traders during each investment phase, supporting and protecting them, so as to allow them to stay on the market for as long as possible.

3.3 – How to invest with brokers

In order to make investments on the Forex and on any other financial market, it is necessary to understand what the evolution of a trend is and to open a position following the hypotheses carried out. However, the trader must understand the dynamics of growth of the trend, and through a well-implemented technical analysis, study the time series, comparing the possible evolutions and reactions of the trends.

The trader must also clearly define their goals. In fact, if for some people trading represents a moment of leisure, for others it has become a real job. This is why it is best for each investor to categorize himself or herself into a certain class, thus also defining his or her own role in Forex.

3.3.1 – CFD

The acronym CFD means the Contract for Difference: the trader can invest in the difference in value of a particular financial instrument, from the moment in which the position in the market is opened to the moment in which it is closed.

This type of investment has involved an increasing number of people, becoming one of the most popular assets in the world. This is because there is no real purchase of securities, and the problem of exchange rates is also eliminated.

3.3.2 – Binary options

Binary options are short and medium-term investment methods. It is simply a matter of opening a position to a certain value of the observed trend and understanding whether the evolution within a well-defined range is up or down. It is a type of investment appreciated precisely because it allows traders to make profits even within a few minutes.

3.3.3 – Forex

Forex is the financial market par excellence. Each broker allows you to open positions in this market, as there is a guarantee of high values of trading volumes and a complete opening, with the consequent possibility of investment, round the clock. The Forex is an unlimited market, both from a temporal and a financial point of view, as it offers greater guarantees of success than any other market.

3.3.4 – Social Trading

The new frontier of trading offers the possibility of combining investment strategies with social networks. In fact, there are platforms that allow traders to make public the strategies implemented, to ask other users for advice on specific processes inherent in them and to share strengths and weaknesses of their analysis with everyone. More and more professional traders decide to subscribe to these social platforms to hone their skills and provide support to all those who come across Forex for the first time.

This methodology also makes it possible to collectively understand certain market processes that can prove to be excessively complex. It is a highly appreciated methodology, which in recent years is spreading more and more, all over the world.

3.3 – Trading platforms

Each broker provides its users with a platform that acts as an interface between the trader and the financial market. Generally, these platforms have various tools, such as charts, oscillators and indicators, able to send signals to the investor, suggesting the opening and closing of positions.

There are both free platforms that can be downloaded directly from the web and paid platforms. The paid platforms differ from the free ones for greater clarity in the offered analysis, a better interpretation of the evolution of the market and a more correct individualization of the possible evolution of the trend.

The platforms are created especially for those who are entering the financial market for the first time and who need to become familiar with the techniques to be used and the strategies to be implemented.

Fundamental Analysis

The origins of Fundamental Analysis date back to ancient times, but despite this, it still represents a fundamental pillar for the study and interpretation of financial assets. Being able to juggle in this type of analysis can be very useful for evaluating the economy and market sectors, to learn to manage and invest prudently and consciously their capital.

Those who intend to invest through the use of Fundamental Analysis but are not professionals in this field can find considerable difficulties. However, thanks to a study of the subject, they may be able to acquire the necessary skills to correctly interpret market signals. In fact, the assumption of this analysis is the interpretation of the data, unlike the Technical Analysis which provides the necessary indicators and resources.

The use of Fundamental Analysis can prove to be an excellent study tool, but it will be even better if it is combined with Technical Analysis in a combined way. The work of the fundamental analyst consists in fact in the research and interpretation of the financial data present in the market, of the indicators and parameters established by the Technical Analysis, to achieve the best possible results.

Chapter 1 - What is Fundamental Analysis

Every investor uses different techniques in order to try to anticipate the movements of the financial markets and thus make profits. One of the techniques most used by traders is called Fundamental Analysis. Regardless of the experience possessed by the investor, the Fundamental Analysis explains, by means of data, what is actually occurring in a given financial market, in such a way to hypothesize what could happen to the trend in subsequent periods.

Many individuals have tried several times to enter the world of trading, but having no real market analysis and money management strategy, they ended their experience with failure. In fact, observing the data provided by research institutions and bodies can prove to be a completely useless action, as the statistics are incomprehensible. An inexperienced trader will not be able to exploit this information, selecting them and inserting them in a logical scheme.

What sets Fundamental Analysis apart from any other market analysis technique is the ability to base one's strategy not on historical or past facts, but on what is happening at the exact moment you decide to invest.

Therefore, the Fundamental Analysis deals with observing and examining the business trend to study its ability to improve in the future and the ways in which it can grow. In this way, the trader has a complete picture of the market trend. Of course, it can be counterproductive to base one's strategy solely on Fundamental Analysis. It is important for a trader to amalgamate the data and statistics deriving from different analysis techniques, in such a way that will increase the chances of making successes in the performance of the trading activity.

However, it is known that many traders decide to completely omit this type of analysis, focusing on other techniques. A new trader that faces the Forex market or any other financial market also using the Fundamental Analysis can start off with other investors, managing to face other competitors and remain active on the market in the long run.

Therefore, Fundamental Analysis does not focus on the visible elements that characterize a trend, such as the price of a specific financial instrument, or on the profits that can be made from a certain investment, but rather it is based on the study of the business and on the value that the same could generate over time, if optimized correctly. This is a much broader view of the market, which makes it possible not to exclude from the analysis of some elements, sometimes fundamental, that otherwise would have been neglected.

The Fundamental Analysis is generally oriented towards the long term, as it is impossible to identify what the trend of the trend may be in the short term, since the business is a very variable datum and prone to seasonal changes, mainly due to the strategies adopted by the companies.

Ultimately, the Fundamental Analysis deals with analyzing and studying what the health status of a given company or a financial asset is. The Fundamental Analysis must be applied in a constant manner, in such a way to verify whether the well-being of the company or if the market is growing or falling and what are the consequences of some economic events on it. The trader must be aware of all the elements that characterize the assets and the economy of the company, but also the performance of the latter, which can only be examined by applying a series of indices to the items that make up the financial statements.

- The Fundamental Analysis aims, according to the company or asset analyzed, a series of objectives, which can help the trader to make the correct investment decisions:
- - First of all, the evaluation of the business, in order to guarantee greater probabilities of profit in the performance of long-term trading;
- - Secondly, the assessment of the macroeconomic trend, with in-depth analysis of the aspects relating to local production, which are able to influence

the performance of the company or asset;

- - Thirdly, the assessment of the administrative and strategic choices of each company capable of influencing the asset, but also of the decisions taken by political leaders with the focus of the effects of these choices on the market;
- - Finally, the detailed evaluation of the relationship between yield and risk, with the study of all the elements that can alter this relationship and with the analysis of future events that could affect it.

1.1 – Main differences between Fundamental Analysis and Technical Analysis

The Fundamental Analysis, for the characteristics and objects taken into consideration, represents the antithesis of Technical Analysis. The latter is used by traders to investigate the historical price trend of a given financial instrument, so as to identify a match in the behavior of the trend, and on the basis of this, hypothesize what its future evolution will be. Therefore, the Technical Analysis does not turn its gaze towards the business and the financial statement ratios but focuses its attention on the prices and the charts that show the fluctuations of the same.

The entire Technical Analysis is based on the concept that all men, and in particular those who act within financial markets, perform their actions repetitively. This idea is linked in particular to the fact that human actions are driven by instinct. When the trend is favorable, uncontrollable euphoria leads subjects to open more and more positions; conversely, the depression due to the inability to anticipate the evolution of the trend leads traders to close positions. These two emotions, completely irrational, are implemented in an almost monotonous manner, pushing the trend up or down. The Technical Analysis tries to understand what the mood of the traders is, so as to anticipate the evolution of the trend.

All this is not contemplated by the Fundamental Analysis, which focuses solely on the data released and made public by the statistical authorities and the financial statements of the individual financial companies. This information, however, is considered incomplete and will have to be analyzed with the help of formulas relating to financial mathematics.

A further distinction between these two types of analysis is represented by the moment in which the entry or exit from the market is decided. In fact, the technical analyst awaits the opening, or closing, of a position until the price has assumed a certain value. This implies that the trader must constantly and almost obsessively observe the trend of the trend and the evolution of the price level. An alternative method is to rely on Trading System, that is automated systems that act completely independently on the financial market on the basis of the strategy set by the investor. The Fundamental Analysis refers to two elements present in the market: the actual value of the asset and the market value. When the actual value is higher than the market value, the fundamental analyst tends to open a position in the market. Vice versa, the position must be closed when the market value exceeds the actual value.

Going deeper into these two different approaches to the market, it is possible to state that the fundamental analyst concentrates his or her forces in the initial phase of trading, namely that of collecting data and studying information, while a greater effort is required from the technical analyst. Moment of observation of the trend, that is during the phase immediately preceding that of entry or exit from the market. In the latter case, however, stress could easily lead the trader to error: the markets are excessively agitated and seizing the right moment to make his choice can be really complicated.

In general, however, it is impossible to define a priori which is the best analysis technique between the two, as both types are linked to external factors and to the risk appetite possessed by the individual investor. An excellent trader is aware of the fact that both Fundamental and Technical Analyses are very important to achieve success in the world of trading and for this reason, the best choice is to use both techniques depending on the situation, or even combine them to increase your chances of making a profit.

Naturally, regardless of the analysis for which one opts, it is fundamental to support each of them with a correct strategy of capital management and risk management. Furthermore, the trader must always take into account the volatility present in the markets, and on the basis of each element make his own choice of investment.

As said, the Technical Analysis and the Fundamental Analysis can be thought of as two opposite categories of market interpretation, but not for this reason, the trader must not use them in a combined manner. In fact, carrying out both types of analysis can bring advantages, as the investor can get a clear idea of the market, both in the short and medium-term, and in the long term.

One of the strategies most used by traders in both Forex and other financial markets is to allocate a certain amount of money on the market and use it following the guidelines indicated in the Technical

Analysis, while the remaining part must be invested according to the concepts inherent in Fundamental Analysis. It is an indirect attempt to reach profitability in the short-term, following the Technical Analysis, and in the long-term, following the Fundamental Analysis.

1.2 – What is the Fundamental Analysis for?

Fundamental Analysis can also be used in areas other than trading. Many managers, for example, use the concepts belonging to this approach to obtain predictions that are probable but not certain on certain economic activities that are somehow related to their company. By broadening the vision of the economic world, it is possible to apply Fundamental Analysis for everyday choices, sometimes even trivial ones, which represent the lives of individuals. In this way, the vision of the future may appear less uncertain and certainly brighter.

Fundamental analysis can also be exploited by individual workers. An employee of a company can analyze the financial statements and all the financial information that must be made public in a mandatory way in order to guess the future of the company in which he or she works and, consequently, his or her future.

Generally, professionals and entrepreneurs can also obtain advantages, anticipating any crisis in the sector. The ability to obtain and understand certain information can allow these subjects to search for differentiation in the market, in such a way to grab as many customers as possible and face the possible crisis in the best way.

Fundamental Analysis can also be used to study the future benefits related to the purchase of a durable good. Whether it is a company or any private entity, the purchase of an asset of this kind must be sufficiently weighted. But an analysis of this kind can also be carried out by a selling company, which studies the financial and economic possibilities of potential customers. Not only that, many physical and juridical subjects analyze the state of health of financial institutions to understand which is the best institution in which to deposit their savings.

To be able to realize all this, however, the Fundamental Analysis must be structured on the basis of some passages, which if carried out correctly, guarantee their full effectiveness.

One of the first steps that every trader or any other person must implement involves the collection of data to be subjected to analysis, relating to a given asset, to a company or a financial institution. Thanks to the advent of the internet, today's subjects are able to find the data necessary to carry out a study of this kind very easily, in particular by browsing the web pages of the various national and international government institutions.

A second step can be identified in the surveys carried out by the interested parties directly in the places of activity. This means that if a trader decides to analyze a particular business in such a way to evaluate the entry into the market, he or she must go to the financial and legal offices of the various companies that characterize this business and verify what the actual influx of customers is, or the breadth of availability of products to sell or even the methods of corporate organization adopted by individual companies.

Once the statistical and visual data are obtained, the fundamental analyst must organize them, subdividing them according to financial nature. Generally, the data are assigned to two categories: the macroeconomic one and the microeconomic one. However, each subject may decide to make a different subdivision according to their needs. To carry out this step, it is necessary to rely on electronic worksheets.

However, the fundamental analyst must continue his or her work of data collection. In fact, it is important to read up on all the competing companies present on the assets to verify what their real state of health is, but above all their attitude. There are indeed market phases during which the companies appear to be aggressive, and deciding to open certain financial positions during these periods can prove counterproductive. The data collected must be used to make comparisons, known to experts as benchmark.

In reality, the data collection phase can be considered infinite for those who decide to rely on Fundamental Analysis. Naturally, once the past and present data of the companies, competitors and financial institutions have been collected, it will only be a work of updating, which involves less effort than that carried out in the initial phase of the study.

Some fundamental analysts, especially if they are inexperienced, decide to skip or otherwise underestimate these steps. In reality, without a statistical basis and a clear view of the market situation and the state of health of competing companies, it is impossible to relate the asset to its market value, to understand if one is in a moment of underestimation or overestimation of the same.

An approach of this kind leads the fundamental analyst to have advantages over any other subject. However, this advantage must be maintained over time, through correct capital management, effective risk management and constant updating of data.

1.3 – Data collection and analysis

As mentioned above, the internet and the various websites represent the main source from which to draw the statistical, patrimonial and economic data useful for achieving a correct Fundamental Analysis. Therefore, it is advisable to mark each individual web page in an economic calendar, in which all the dates of publication of the information necessary for analysis are reported.

In particular, the fundamental analyst must search for all the monetary policy announcements, relating to data or information, which are periodically released by the individual national central banks. Furthermore, the quarterly data relating to the GDP trend, that is the Gross Domestic Product, of each nation, which indicates the health status and the economic evolution, are fundamental. Finally, depending on the type of Fundamental Analysis carried out, it is necessary to collect data relating to the production of the manufacturing sector only and, consequently, of all the production that does not derive from this sector, in particular, that relating to the industrial sector and the service sector or services. But not only. It is important not to underestimate the data relating to inflation in a given State, an element that greatly conditions the price trend on the various assets, but also those that refer to the employment and welfare of a country. Finally, the fundamental analyst must collect the data that allow to obtain the indices representative of the trust of companies and consumers, the data reported on the balance sheets of companies or other economic and patrimonial data that are released by the institutions or by the companies in a periodic manner, such as the data relating to forecasts on future market trends that are issued by the European Commission.

It is also advisable to find pure statistics and data, which have not already been analyzed and interpreted by the press, as the business or asset situation may have been altered, even unintentionally. Other times the difficulty of finding information is linked to the difference in language, especially if it involves investments to be made in Asian countries. So if you are not able to interpret a language, an investment of this kind could turn out to be really very dangerous, not having a Fundamental Analysis of support and a well-studied strategy behind it.

The creation of an economic calendar, therefore, represents one of the first necessary steps in order to organize one's data collection activity. You can download already compiled calendars online, but they will have to be updated and increased based on your needs.

Once a calendar of this kind has been created, it is possible to analyze the various macroeconomic and microeconomic data present in each individual asset.

1.3.1 – Macroeconomic data

Macroeconomics is considered a branch of financial matter that deals with the analysis of some basic measures to carry out a correct fundamental analysis.

First of all, macroeconomics is concerned with assessing the relationship between national debt and Gross Domestic Product, to understand the actual evolutionary trend of a State.

Secondly, macroeconomics considers what the national employment rate is. This rate can be broken down by age and by seasonal period in order to carry out different investigations. The rate of inflation is also one of the basic indicators of Fundamental Analysis. This rate must be relatively low to prevent the currency from losing value, but not too low as a State with an inflation rate that tends to zero risks ending up in a recession. Finally, macroeconomics deals with the rate of economic growth, which shows the extent to which a country can obtain benefits in the future and achieve certain objectives.

Each of these rates or ratios allows the fundamental analyst to assess the course of a given economic reality. However, macroeconomics does not refer to individual activities, but to markets considered as aggregate systems. Therefore, the analyst is required to combine the individual company outputs in order to guess what the economic evolution in a given asset may be. The analysis must be carried out considering the pure data, not processed by other bodies or agencies.

There are numerous reports, also available online, which offer some interpretations of asset trends. However, these interpretations may prove to be inaccurate, and for this reason, it is important to rely on one's own skills rather than on those made available by external parties. Furthermore, these reports can refer to time horizons different from those set by the analyst. In this sense, the interpretations will be different, being based on completely different logics.

In this logic, it becomes important to divide the trade into two components: the liquid capital, represented by payments and receipts, and the deferred capital, represented by investments, credits, and debts. In addition to this, the analyst must also evaluate the national balance of payments, to see if the value of exports exceeds that of imports.

However, fundamental analysts can use systems that simplify data and economic reality. In particular, there are two models that perform this task effectively, namely Investment Saving - Liquidity Money, known with the acronym IS-LM, and the Aggregate Supply - Aggregate Demand, known more simply as AD-AS. The first of these two models has the task of identifying which is the balance point on an economic level, considering this level to determine the starting pointto make forecasts in the medium term. The second model, on the other hand, focuses attention on the individual processes that bring the market to a certain equilibrium point and tries to understand why these processes occur. However, it is wrong to exclude completely from the analysis obtained with these models the fluctuations that characterize the market in the short term. In fact, these are very important to be able to define the trend in the market in wider horizons.

Therefore, the analysis of macroeconomic data is fundamental to understand what is the evolution of some assets or of an entire financial market, but also of much wider economic realities. An analysis based on this information can lead to surprising results, which can confirm or contradict the results of microeconomic analysis, but which nonetheless offers very important interpretations to understand what the market trend may be in the long term. It also considers some unexpected events.

The advantage of Fundamental Analysis of macroeconomic data is represented by the possibility of easily and at any time receiving information and data relating to the economic realities observed.

1.3.2 – Microeconomics data

Microeconomics stands in contrast to macroeconomics, as it analyzes individual economic realities, evaluating their evolution over time. In particular, microeconomics studies and focuses on trends in the market of single individuals, understood as consumers of goods produced by companies and services offered by them, but also of individual companies, in the dual role of suppliers and customers, and finally organizations and public and private institutions.

It is important for the fundamental analyst to understand that macroeconomic data do not have a real meaning unless they are accompanied by microeconomic ones. If a single company, even if rather large, dismisses some of its employees, this choice will have no repercussions on macroeconomic data. At the same time, however, if the layoffs concern several companies, then the employment rate, understood as a macroeconomic quantity will be influenced by varying its value.

In any case, it is always good to compare and integrate the data held, in such a way to understand in greater detail what the current market trend is.

The fundamental analysts study the microeconomic data knowing a concept that is at the base of this environment, that is what the subjects carry out every single action searching for profit. So every company sells a certain product within the market at a price that is certainly higher than the sum of the individual costs incurred to produce it. If this does not happen, the company will face a loss, and in the microeconomic world, this cannot be accepted. Loss-making companies are destined to leave the market. Once they reach a certain threshold, they are no longer able to sustain the expenses. Therefore, investors will be required to select only those investments that guarantee a sufficient probability of gain in the long term, while they will have to resist the temptation to make some investments just following their own instincts.

This temptation, which often results in bankruptcy investments, arise in delicate moments crossed by traders. They have chosen the wrong business to entrust their money to and try to remedy the initial mistake by increasing the risk of their investment.

1.4 – Operational difficulties in applying the Fundamental Analysis

The difficulties deriving from the application of the Fundamental Analysis mean that there are many who despise it in favor of Technical Analysis. But in reality, this complexity is the reason most of these people are unable to use this type of analysis. In fact, if in the Technical Analysis, it is sufficient to study the various indicators and become familiar with them, in the Fundamental Analysis, it is essential to interpret the signals on the basis of the economic, financial and social variables that can intervene in a given context or market. This interpretation is operationally very complex as it goes beyond logic, and it is not easy to manage not to be conditioned by emotions in favor of rationality. A rumor is enough to influence the market and prices.

Therefre, the interpretation represents the main operational difficulty of the Fundamental Analysis, and becomes even more complex due to the high number of data to be analyzed, quantifiable in thousands of thousands of indicators, which could influence and positively or negatively affect prices. To overcome this problem, fundamental analysts try to circumscribe the most important data to facilitate at least part of the entire analysis procedure.

The Fundamental Analysis deals with the study of the macroeconomic and microeconomic reference environment based on a well-defined econometric model that identifies the relationships between the analyzed economic realities. However, these models are not flexible, or rather only if they are applied in decisions regarding the choices of national economic policy made by governments. If they are used to operate in the financial markets, such models are not easily adaptable as they are composed of variables that cannot be controlled over time and because of their specificity towards one market rather than another. Furthermore, due to the amount of data to be adapted, the signals will not be timely.

For this reason, it is necessary to havean in-depth knowledge of mathematics, the market, econometrics, and a marked predisposition for the interpretation of data.

Sector and company analyze also present difficulties in identifying the possible financial, economic and equity scenarios of companies to estimate the income flows related to equities in the most correct way. To do this, those who decide to invest in the market using Fundamental Analysis can use supports, free or paid, that provide information, but which are however far from what is offered by the various brokers.

Various websites have been created around the world that provide a useful database for those who want to make online trading operations in an informed way, such as Financialweb, but in Europe, there are still no such sites.

The knowledge of financial analysis is a prerequisite for Fundamental Analysis, made starting from the company balance sheets and the market, through the various indices of appreciation, but the brokers rarely offer tools of this type. Therefore, the only way to correctly implement the Fundamental Analysis is to become good fundamental analysts.

Chapter 2 - The financial statements and the Fundamental Analysis

The Fundamental Analysis is based on one of the main tools used in the entire economic environment, that is the financial statements. The main purpose of this document is to show all stakeholders, internal and external, the economic and financial performance of the company. It reacts to a sort of guarantee that the company shows to every potential customer or investor. Furthermore, this document allows the company that prepares it to manage its business properly. However, it is a legal obligation for listed companies to prepare and publish the financial statements, which must be made available to each individual investor or interested party. Furthermore, the opening of companies to international markets has obliged the law to attempt to standardize these information documents to facilitate a comparison between the financial statements of different companies or between the financial statements of the same company in different periods. Of course, a comparison of this kind can only be made between companies in the same sector.

In reality, many fundamental analysts fail to carry out an analysis based on the balance sheet, as they often do not have the necessary skills to read the indices in the most appropriate way, misinterpreting the company's performance. At other times, the balance sheet can be drafted in a rather confusing manner, which removes potential investors.

In order to understand more quickly the state of health of a given economic reality, it is useful to focus on three documents of the financial statements, namely the Balance Sheet, the Income Statement and the financial statement ratios.

2.1 – Budget structure

The Balance Sheet and the Income Statement are the main documents of the financial statements and are accompanied, in order to be explained and integrated by the Explanatory Note and the Cash Flow Statement.

The Balance Sheet presents a structure with opposite sections. In the first part, that is to the left of the prospectus, are the activities; on the right, there are the liabilities. The total of the two sections must correspond to have a correct Balance Sheet.

The income statement, on the other hand, has a scalar form, divided into four sections. As we proceed in the preparation of the Income Statement, various fundamental elements are highlighted to be able to proceed with analyzing the financial statements using the indicators.

Both the Balance Sheet and the Income Statement must then be reclassified, so as to highlight further elements, which in the previous draft could not be shown.

2.1.1 – Balance Sheet

The Balance Sheet deals with grouping all the active and passive elements of a company. The active elements include investments, fixed assets, whether they be tangible, intangible or financial, current assets, consisting of inventories, receivables, and cash. Among the passive elements, on the other hand, are the shareholders' equity, the provisions for risks and charges, the severance pay and the debts. In addition to these elements, accruals and deferrals must also be appropriately divided between assets and liabilities depending on the financial event.

The net assets will be the result of the difference between active and passive elements. In this way, the interested party will be able to understand what the actual business value is once all the debts recorded in the financial statements have been settled. Therefore, the net assets show how much equity the company owns for the realization of a production phase, and by exclusion, how much are the external sources of financing owned by the company. Naturally, a healthy company must act relying only on the capital already in its possession, without relying on loans or financing received from credit institutions.

Therefore, the final objective of the Balance Sheet of the financial statements is to highlight both the capital structure and the financial situation of a particular company. It is for this reason that the balance sheet is considered as one of the main documents that must necessarily be examined by fundamental analysts.

2.1.2 – Income Statement

The Income Statement is composed of all the items relating to costs and revenues that have occurred in a specific period of time, which generally coincides with a calendar year. By observing the Profit and Loss Account, it is possible to guess whether the company has made a profit during the financial year, that is if it is a profitable company, or if it has incurred losses. In rare cases, the company closes the budget with a draw, that is with perfect equality between costs and revenues.

Defining how much profit or loss a company has is very simple. It is necessary to add revenues and costs algebraically. If a positive value is obtained, that is if the revenues exceed the costs, then there is a profit; vice versa, if the revenues are lower than the costs, there will be loss.

However, the Income Statement provides many other interesting data for the potential investor. First of all, it is possible to break down the economic results according to the product or the company production sector. In this way, it is possible to guess which product is considered the company's flagship, the new products launched on the market and even the weak points of the company. Furthermore, through the Income Statement, it is possible to analyze the company assets, comparing them with the profits made.

Another aspect linked to the Income Statement is the ability to demonstrate to all interested parties the quality of the work performed by each individual manager, depending on the functions performed. The management aspects of an enterprise are one of the most important and at the same time the most underestimated aspects within an asset. In reality, the actual performance of a company depends on the ideas and strategies implemented by these subjects. These strategies will have to deal with customers, suppliers and above all, competitors, and lead the company to optimize profit. But the goal is not always achieved.

The main difference between the Balance Sheet and the Income Statement is that the former offers a static view of a company's assets, that is, asseststhat are held at the time the financial statements are drawn up and therefore at the end of the year, while the latter analyzes and represents an economic situation evolving during the year, that is, the income stream.

2.1.3 – Notes to the financial statements and cash flow statement

Although less important for the achievement of the objectives set by a fundamental analyst, the financial statements also comprise two other documents, namely the Notes to the Financial Statements and the Financial Statement.

The Notes to the Financial Statements show all the parties involved how to implement the financial statements and what the principles adopted in it are. It also has the function of explaining individual items in a timely and detailed manner. Therefore, this document plays a fundamental role in the standardization of financial statements. In fact, the principles on which a budget is drawn up are different and follow completely different approaches and logic, depending on their vision of the market and the economy. Therefore, it is opportune to specify which of these ways the managers have adopted for the realization of the budget and how each item must be interpreted by the interested subjects.

The Financial Statement, on the other hand, is a document that in Italy has become mandatory only in the year 2015, but which nevertheless plays an important role in the interpretation of the financial statements. Its objective is to describe the liquid assets, breaking them down and analyzing them, in such a way to offer a clear and lucid vision both on the amount and on their evolution, as the values present at the beginning and end of the year are indicated. In addition, the Financial Statement analyzes the financial flows deriving from the individual company sectors, specifically from that relating to the operating activity, from the investment sectors, and from the financing sectors. The importance of this document is to guarantee the fundamental analyst a dynamic view of corporate income. Indeed, the stock of assets, static, does not allow us to investigate the trend and performance of the company in the market, and therefore offers only a limited analysis of the state of health of the company. Therefore, it is necessary to deepen the flows and analyze them in detail, in order to guess what the real business trend may be.

Furthermore, the preparation of the financial statements is based on the application of certain principles established by national law or by international regulation. The most important are those relating to prudence, which implies that only certain positive components must be reported in the financial statements, while negative ones can also be presumed; to the economic competence, which implies that only the charges and revenues pertaining to the financial year must be entered, regardless of the moment in which they will have financial manifestation; the prevalence of the substance over the form, based on which it is necessary to take into account the economic function of the individual items.

2.2 – Analysis of the financial statement indicators useful for Fundamental Analysis

The budget analysis is a very complex step, which requires technical skills and in-depth knowledge of the subject. The purpose is to obtain information that otherwise cannot be known: in particular, it involvess data concerning the management of the company. The analysis focuses on the items present in the Balance Sheet and the Income Statement relating to the year in closing and offers important indications, very useful to the fundamental analyst, which reveal the true state of health of the company. To be able to use them, however, it is necessary to re-elaborate and reclassify the financial statements according to various methods, depending on the aim pursued and the elements that we intend to investigate.

2.2.1 - Earning Before Interest, Taxes, Depreciation and Amortization

The first important financial statement indicator is called the Earning Before Interest, Taxes, Depreciation and Amortization, better known with the acronym EBITDA. The aim is to offer the fundamental analyst an objective view of the amount of wealth that has been produced by the company, only in its characteristic sector, namely the main one. It is also known as Gross Operating Margin, or simply as MOL. In reality, this indicator exploits the reclassification of the Income Statement according to the Added Value criterion to obtain an intermediate result, the result of which is solely the operational management, without the interest expense, taxes, depreciation and amortization being still covered.

An advantage offered by the calculation of the EBITDA is represented by the possibility of easily comparing the Gross Operating Margin of a financial statement with that present in the other financial statements, so as to immediately have a clear vision of the company that shows the best operating performance. In fact, the standardization of EBITDA has been carried out over the years precisely to favor a comparison by investors, but also by fundamental analysts, who base their profits on the study of company characteristics.

2.2.2 – Return On Equity

The Return On Equity indicator, better known as ROE, is one of the return on equity ratios. This indicator is used to analyze the profitability of a company in percentage terms, as it compares Net Income to Net Capital. Therefore, it indicates how much percentage of investment has translated into income. To get real information on the performance of the company, however, it is necessary to compare the value of the ROE obtained with the various investment indicators to be able to identify the opportunity cost linked to the initial investment of the company. The difference arising from this comparison is defined in the economic sphere as a risk premium. If this assumes a value of zero, then it means that it would be useless to invest in that company, as the investor would obtain the same result by not making any investment.

2.2.3 – Return On Investment

The Return On Investment indicator, also known as the ROI acronym, aims to highlight the economic efficiency of a particular company, taking into consideration only the management characteristic. The ROI does not consider the sources that are used to reach the income produced during the year. Consequently, this indicator is used by fundamental analysts to understand what the return on invested capital is.

To achieve its objective, the ROI compares the total operating result obtained by the company with the average of the capital invested during the same period.

However, the fundamental analyst must take into account certain defects in this indicator. First of all, the ROI increases with the passing of the financial years, as the balance sheet will always suffer more from the increase in the value of depreciation. A second negative point concerning ROI is that it relates a stock value, that is, the invested capital, to a flow, that is, the operating income produced.

Chapter 3 - Fundamental Analysis in the stock market and Forex

The Fundamental Analysis and the Technical Analysis represent the best methodologies to analyze the evolution of the financial markets and, in particular, of the Forex market. Without these two approaches, traders would not have a solid basis on which to make their predictions, and investments could prove bankrupt. Traders rely in particular on Fundamental Analysis to try to predict what the trend of a given trend may be in the long run.

Naturally, the Fundamental Analysis carried out on the financial markets will focus attention on the price levels of financial instruments, securities and currencies present in the market on which the trader intends to invest. It is natural, however, that an analysis of this kind can only be carried out by an experienced trader or by real analysts who carry out these studies by profession. This is because inexperienced investors do not have sufficient skills to correctly describe the economic events that can affect the financial market.

Generally, the Fundamental Analysis applied on the financial markets focuses on the macroeconomic causes, that is, on all those events able to modify the curve of the demand and that of the offer even in the largest financial market in the world, namely the Forex. Thus the fundamental analyst turns his or her gaze towards the progress of the individual nations, but also towards a homogeneous trend that can bring together a group of states that have similar geographical, ethnic or cultural features, or towards the entire world economic evolution. However, what mostly influences the financial market are the decisions taken by national and international political leaders. In fact, they have direct influences on the economic results of the individual states, since the correlation between the world of politics and that of finance is direct. Further aspects that affect the fundamental analysis are the impacts of the social world and even of the climate, both on trade and on the price of goods. These are aspects that should not be underestimated, which can often help the trader to understand in advance the future market swings, thus generating more profits.

3.1 – The stock market: sector analysis and company valuation

One of the objectives of a fundamental analyst is to understand what the real value of the shares is, in order to compare it with the value expressed on the market. In this way, the trader has the opportunity to invest in undervalued securities, assuming that they will soon take their real value, thanks to the classic financial corrections of the market. The Fundamental Analysis approach to the stock market is based on a series of steps that every investor must put into practice.

The first phase refers to the analysis of all the macroeconomic scenarios that can influence the stock market. First of all, this analysis must be subdivided by geographical area and by economic area. In this way, the trader can opt for the markets considered more favorable, depending on the results of the analysis.

The second phase involves sectoral analysis. This is a complex study, as it considers all the businesses present on the market in which it has chosen to invest and examines all possible future scenarios. The sectoral analysis goes beyond the world strictly linked to the economy and finance, as it encompasses social, IT, political and cultural subjects. Of course, to carry out an analysis of this kind, one requires certain skills and a thorough knowledge of the stock market.

The third and final phase involves the evaluation of the companies present on the market. This means that the trader must evaluate the financial statements made public by each company, must reclassify the Balance Sheet and the Income Statement and on these statements must apply the financial statement ratios. In this way, the investor will be able to understand what the real value of the company is. This value must then be compared to the quotation that the company expresses on the market, and on the difference arising from it, the trader will be able to make an investment with a much higher probability of a positive outcome.

3.2 – The intrinsic value of equities

One of the most important steps in the whole Fundamental Analysis is for a trader to understand what it means to analyze the intrinsic value of a given asset. The definition of intrinsic value takes on a rather simple meaning to understand from a theoretical point of view, but in practice, it can be very difficult to obtain.

However, it is necessary to start from the assumption that the intrinsic value of a given financial instrument or of a certain asset is a conceptually utopian value. In fact, this value would be possible In reality only if all investors were totally rational subjects, who do not make mistakes and who efficiently act on perfect benchmarks. Only in this way, in fact, could the actual value of a financial product or a market be obtained.

Identifying this value is however possible, at least hypothetically, and it is above all extremely advantageous. To do this, a fundamental analyst should sift through a business in every area, from the management to the strategies adopted, from the investments made to the financial statements, taking into account the sources from which the financial resources are drawn and their ability to turn into income. Once the analyst has an idea of what the intrinsic price of a certain economic reality may be, he or she will have to analyze the value it has assumed on the market and based on this, he or she will have to make his or her own investment. The basic concept on which to base his or her trading, however, is that in the long term the price taken by a financial asset and its intrinsic value will tend to coincide. So if the value assumed in the market by the business is lower than the calculated intrinsic value, then the analyst will be oriented to buying the stock, knowing that probably in the long run these will correspond.

Therefore, it is possible to affirm that the determination of the intrinsic value of a stock or asset can represent the main objective of the entire Fundamental Analysis. Once the investor has become aware of this data, in fact, he or she may decide to make his or her own investment or not, knowing already, if it has been correctly counted, what the probable future trend of the price observed in the market will be.

It is for this reason that the experts in the field have tried to create different models that help the investor to trace more quickly to the intrinsic value. Some models, however, involve rather complex passages, which can lead to error and to obtain a completely inaccurate result.

However, it is possible to bring the models back to only two types: the Dividend Discount Models, also known as dividend discounting models, and the Stock Market Multiples, known as models of market multiples. Each of these models has undergone important changes over the years, which have led to an overall optimization of the entire Fundamental Analysis.

3.2.1 - The dividend discounting model

The Dividend Discount Models focus on the discounting of the final price of a specific financial instrument and on the discounting of all dividends that have been paid in a given time interval, which coincides with the period of ownership of the same instrument. This discounting inevitably depends on an interest rate, which must be calculated by relying on additional analysis tools, such as the CAPM model (Capital Asset Pricing Model).

The logic that characterizes this model is based on the knowledge and the study of balance sheet data made public by the companies, from which it is possible to infer a hypothetical intrinsic value of financial security. The value obtained is to be compared with that on the market, both to understand if it is actually reliable, and to guess whether the business is undervalued or overvalued.

3.2.2 – The market multiples method

The same results obtained with the dividend discounting method can also be reached with the market multiples method, which is one of the most used methods by traders to make a correct business valuation. This system bases its approach on the valuation of the prices of goods produced by similar companies belonging to the same sector. The prices analyzed are related to the items in the financial statements, in particular, the profit, but also to the EBITDA, EBIT and shareholders' equity. From this relationship, different multiples arise.

The most important and most used multiple by traders is relative to the ratio between price and the average profit of the sector. Generally, the historical profit is used, but the best indication is obtained by comparing the price to the expected profit for the current year. This market multiple provides important information regarding the number of years necessary to repay with just the profits the investments made by the company. A low value of the report indicates that the company is undervalued, conversely high values indicate that there is an overvaluation. However, there is no standard value that the trader can consider as an optimal point, but the evaluation of the multiple must be compared with the reference sector. In fact, a mature sector has lower price-earnings ratios while, due to the great expectations of growth, the young sectors have a much higher average ratio.

Also multiple refers to the relationship between price and equity. It is possible to obtain the net assets both from the difference between assets and liabilities and by adding the reserves indicated in the statement to the share capital. This business valuation method is generally used to analyze the real value held by financial, insurance or banking companies. This report helps the trader to understand the price at which the market is willing to pay a surplus with respect to the value of the company assets.

If the report gives a result lower than 1, then the company is undervalued and therefore a lower value is expressed on the market than the real one. If, on the other hand, the value generates a value of less than 0.5, the company's valuation is very bad and the multiple even indicates a high risk of a real crisis.

3.3 – The real estate sector

One of the main indicators of the state of health of a market is certainly the real estate sector. This represents one of the most abundant sources from which a trader can draw a lot of information, especially in relation to long-term investments.

The importance of the real estate sector is derived mainly from the massive influence it expresses both at the macroeconomic level and at the microeconomic level. In particular, the first is one of the main indicators of the development perspectives that an economy can conceal, while the second is an indicator of the portfolio values present among private individuals.

Generally, the real estate sector considers real estate as an evaluation unit, made up of both land and a building erected on it. However, the assessment ignores this consideration and focuses attention on the intended use, that is, it evaluates whether the property is for commercial use or simply residential.

As with almost any other asset, even in the real estate sector, it is possible to make long-term investments, or speculative investments to be converted into profits in the short and medium term. In particular, an investor speculates in the real estate sector by buying a property at a lower price than its real value, which can happen for example during a real estate auction, and then resell the same property at the right price, in the shortest possible time.

What further links the real estate sector with the financial market is the provision of credits. In fact, the purchase, construction or renovation of a property are the main reasons why a funding body grants a loan to a private individual, while the purchase or realization of productive properties is the basic reason for the granting of corporate mortgages or for the stipulation of leasing contracts. It is because of the close link between real estate and interest expense, property prices are subject to strong volatility, a characteristic that can have significant influences on the stock market. In fact, banks and credit institutions have a variable reserve, linked to the quality of the credits that are provided. Any devaluations on the real estate market can generate very negative consequences, which can lead to even very serious financial crises, such as that occurred in the United States in 2009.

Therefore, a fundamental analyst must constantly monitor the entire real estate sector in order to understand which events can affect the financial markets and which ones can have only relative effects. To facilitate this task, each state has created a system that constantly monitors the real estate sector. These systems allow you to acquire certain periodic information, monthly or quarterly depending on the country, on the various municipalities, cities, urban conglomerates, and metropolitan cities. With this data, the analyst can more easily and more precisely guess what the current price trend is within the market and can create forecasts about its possible future developments.

The organization that plays this role in the United States is the S&P Case, while in the European territory, the Eurostat provides the necessary data. In Japan, the studymade available to all potential analysts, traders and investors is carried out directly by the Ministry that deals with both the territorial situation and the infrastructures. The latter has divided the analysis of the real estate market into two different categories: the first is dedicated exclusively to in-depth analyses carried out on the market, but also to the interpretations relating to the trends of the various trends, while the second is dedicated to pure statistical data.

To open an investment of real estate type, it is possible to adopt two different types of execution. The first is direct and requires a rather large capital reserve and constant and active management of the investment. The allocated capital can be either own or derived from loans or loans granted. The second method involves the possibility of buying the property without holding the pure property, but only a portion of a fund. For many reasons, the use of mutual funds differs from the first. In fact, this second way of opening an investment requires much less time and much less dedication. Furthermore, the costs related to the management and to the various commissions related to the project will be divided according to the quota held. Another advantage is a possibility of dividing the risk. In fact, a real estate fund of this kind involves the subdivision of capital over a very large number of assets, thus also favoring the possibility of investing in foreign markets that are also very distant.

In addition to direct information, the real estate sector also offers some indirect information, which must be received and examined by the fundamental analyst. In fact, the real estate indexes can be used as real benchmarks, constituting a very interesting basis of analysis to guess what the future trends of the various financial instruments observed may be.

3.4 – Fundamental Analysis in Forex

Even in Forex, fundamental analysts have the objective of understanding what the future trend in the prices of financial instruments in the market may be. In order to achieve this goal, however, it is necessary to take into account different aspects, which constantly affect the market and which sanction the path followed by financial trends.

One of the first aspects that every fundamental analyst must necessarily study is the interest rate. The value of this element is decided by the central banks of each nation, which acts according to the logic adopted by the various governments. Therefore, it is inevitable that the choices made in this area have some influence on the Forex market, especially if it is a state that has some influence at the world level.

Inflation is another element that should not be underestimated. This quantifies the value and the purchasing power of money and is, therefore, a fundamental aspect of every financial market. Also, in this case, the governments, through different maneuvers, influence the rate of inflation, knowing that a high rate leads to a halt in consumption, while an excessively low rate leads to recession.

Naturally, every fundamental analyst who acts in the Forex market must necessarily relate to the national Gross Domestic Product. Analyzing this element is indispensable in order to understand what the level of volatility on the market is. Moreover, GDP is considered one of the most important indicators of the economic performance of a nation. Fundamental analysts can also use preliminary GDP ratios, without waiting for the official report, in order to anticipate a possible trend reversal, obtaining substantial profits.

But Forex also has its roots in society, and for this reason, the unemployment rate is one of the most influential indicators of financial instrument price trends. In addition to representing another important indicator of the health status of a nation, the unemployment rate also outlines the average wealth held by individual citizens, which affect national consumption and GDP.

A nation with excellent social and economic welfare also shows a positive trade balance, obtained from the difference between imports and exports made in a given period. Moreover, if imports exceed exports, the value of the currency is strengthened, while in the opposite case the currency will be weakened.

Even the stability of governments is one of the main elements that determine the fluctuations within Forex. Naturally, the trust placed by individual traders in domestic financial stocks causes prices to fluctuate.

In addition to all these indicators and situations, each trader will have to focus his or her financial analysis on three other elements. These in fact, directly and indirectly, influence the market and require a detailed and non-negligible examination.

3.4.1 – The Monetary Policy of the Central Banks

The analysis of the Monetary Policy moves implemented by the individual central banks is fundamental to understand the real possibilities that within a state a tendency towards economic growth can be generated. The Monetary Policy does not only act in the sphere of inflation and interest rates but also deals with the relationship with other states, technology, investments, and even social welfare. Therefore, it is a very broad discipline that embraces almost every aspect of the economy. However, every decision is taken and implemented by the individual central banks, which act by virtue of the political orientation present to the government and following the guidelines of the international central banks.

3.4.2 – The economy

Traders must also base their analysis on the dynamics that determine the economic performance of a nation or group of nations. This type of analysis must be based on all the social and political factors that characterize a territory, but also on the level of national consumption and the various productive sectors. Therefore, the economy is one of the pillars that support the entire Fundamental Analysis of Forex and, in order to analyze it in-depth, the trader will have to devote a lot of time to this phase of the analysis, or rely on data that are already ready, but which could turn out to be misinterpreted or incomplete.

3.4.3 – The trend in gold and oil commodities

Gold and oil are the commodities that most influence the financial sector and the Forex market. They are two elements often underestimated, neglected and not understood within the analysis, but in reality, they are crucial to understanding what the future trend of the trends may be.

In fact, gold is considered the refuge good par excellence. This means that traders, in the event that the markets go through some negative phases, try to invest in gold. For this reason, therefore, while all financial instruments show a negative trend, gold appears to be the only element to present a positive trend. Conversely, gold shows a downward trend when the market is experiencing moments of euphoria.

Oil is also one of the commodities that most influence the markets around the world and in particular the Forex. There are two different types of oil, but the advice is to focus attention on West Texas Intermediate, also known as WTI, which has a greater influence than Brent.

In fact, almost all world economies depend on oil, either because they import it or because they export it, and consequently this importance inevitably spills over into the financial market. A drop in oil prices, therefore, would entail advantages for importing countries and a disadvantage for exporting countries, and vice versa.

Conclusions

The topics discussed so far have allowed us to learn the main notions of Fundamental Analysis and what it entails. It is based on a series of simple principles, but difficult to apply if you do not have the necessary skills. To undertake the Fundamental Analysis, it is important to learn to examine the data of the financial statements of the companies to be able to make estimates and forecasts of short, medium and long term. The collection and the study of the great amount of financial data require quite long times and valid knowledge of the market and of the mathematical and econometric disciplines, which is why the Fundamental Analysis is not easy to use by the less experienced. But, if used correctly, it can guarantee optimal and optimized management of its capital, in such a way that it is invested by reducing risks and based on market volatility, with awareness and avoiding making wrong choices that would lead to the loss of money.

The cardinal principles of Fundamental Analysis are also useful for technical analysts as support tools in investment decisions, thanks to the study of the calendar of macroeconomic events to establish what is the most appropriate time to make investments.

Therefore, the Fundamental Analysis is a valid instrument, even if it presents some limits connected to its complexity, but it remains however very important to fully understand the financial markets.

Operating Forex Trading

The Forex market is the largest financial market in the world, in which currency swaps are made every day for millions of dollars. This is a fair market, not controllable by any institution or government, which changes exclusively in relation to fluctuations in exchange rates. Forex trading consists of buying a currency the moment it sells another, as currency quotes are formed by pairs, such as the Euro-Dollar pair. In the pair, the two currencies take on different roles, one indicates the base currency, while the other represents the quoted currency. The fundamental element that unites them is the exchange price.

The Forex market, as well as that of trading in general, attracts more and more investors. However, there is a great deal of confusion in this, as there is a substantial difference between Forex and stock trading. Forex is a market based on currency trading, while stock trading is based on trading in securities such as stocks or bonds on the stock exchange. Compared to stock trading, Forex has more flexible opening hours, has reduced fees to attract more investors, provides a relatively limited number of currency pairs to facilitate the choice of traders, and does not have any restrictions. Another point in favor of the Forex market is the total absence of intermediaries, with the consequent reduction of platform management costs, which only serve to connect with the market.

The choice between the two investment systems is not simple, especially if you do not have experience in the sector, but to undertake both roads, it is always advisable to carry out a careful study work, with constancy and commitment, because only with sacrifice will it be possible to obtain positive results.

Forex trading is able to guarantee greater stability in relation to the events that can influence the market, so starting to invest its capital in it could prove to be an apt move, but it is fundamental never to lose sight of the limits and the rules of good sense and prudence.

Chapter 1 - What is Forex Trading

The Forex is a market that includes within it all the exchanges of a financial nature that take place between the various subjects, in particular between funding bodies and traders. For this reason, Forex, also known as the currency market, is considered the largest financial market on the entire planet. Itderived its name from the union of two words: the first is Foreign which literally means "foreigner", while the second is Exchange So Forex is nothing but a market based on the exchange of foreign currencies. The numbers relating to the 230

Forex market are truly incredible: every day, the exchange of cash made within it amounts to over 5 trillion US dollars.

One of its main features, which distinguishes it from any other stock market in the world, is its lack of hourly limits, as it is possible to trade at any time throughout the day and night. This aspect should not be underestimated: traders can exploit the consequences generated by international events in real-time, whether they are related to politics, society or the economy.

What also distinguishes the Forex is the total absence of a financial center. This means that the prices relating to the financial instruments traded within it simply react to the market according to the normal law of supply and demand. On the interpretation of this mechanism, traders must act promptly, who will play upwards in the event that the demand for the product observed increases, or downward in the opposite case. The absence of a real headquarters has led Forex to be known worldwide as an "over the counter" market.

1.1 – How Forex is born

The emergence of the Forex market can be traced back to 1944, following the agreements of Bretton Woods, in New Hampshire, between the USA, France and the United Kingdom. This meeting had the purpose of strengthening the individual economies of the participating states, through an international monetary policy, which included the insertion of well-defined procedures and rules. The Forex is the first market in the world, the result of political negotiation, created with the aim of regulating economic relations between the various world nations.

Two projects were presented to reconstruct the monetary and financial system: the first, called White Project, was presented by the American Harry Dexter White, the second, called Keynes Project, was presented by the Englishman John Maynard Keynes. The White Project was focused on the formation of a new body that was supposed to finance all member countries on the basis of the shares of capital subscribed by each of them, in a system based on the US dollar. The Keynes Project foresaw the institution of a new currency, called Bancor, with which the various countries would have had to compensate their debts and credits, based on their economic weight in international trade estimated as the average of the last three years. A compromise emerged between the two projects, but the Piano White gained more weight.

The first fundamental consequence was the establishment of the International Monetary Fund and the World Bank, as institutions with functions of support and supervision over the world economy. In addition, the Bretton Woods agreements for the first time sanctioned the replacement of the British pound with the US dollar as the reference currency for the exchange rate. The value of the dollar was anchored to that of gold: one ounce was priced at $ 35. The states adhering to these agreements had the obligation to control national currency fluctuations with respect to the Dollar, keeping them below a percentage point.

The most significant years for Forex werethose between 1950 and 1960. In these years, a large number of operators entered the market and the volume of trade increased considerably.

The monetary system that came into being as a result of the Bretton Woods agreements proved to be efficient since its establishment until the early 1970s. The established rules allowed to achieve the set objectives and to regularize the market, preventing the formation of conflicts. In these years, the United States had to face events that significantly affected national public spendings, such as the war in Vietnam and the expensive Great Society social program. In this situation, public indebtedness coincided with the increase in investors' conversion requests for gold reserves. For this reason, in the summer of 1971, President Nixon decided to suspend this convertibility sanctioned by the previous agreements, announcing this decision at Camp David. Thus at the end of 1971, the G10 finally put an end to the system created following the Bretton Woods agreements. The system dictated by the Smithsonian Agreement, based on flexible exchange rates, began with the necessary devaluation of the US dollar and the consequent fluctuation of exchange rates. The establishment of the new monetary system, with the obvious abatement of the previous one did not lead to the disposal of the institutions founded in 1944, which, outside the GATT, continue to exist today.

The years following the announcement of Camp David are characterized by the leading role of international banks and technology in Forex. In particular, the latter allowed, starting from 1980, to increase trading volumes, thanks to the increase in speed and the expansion of operating hours. The costs and the commissions connected to the trading operations appeared as an obstacle for many insurmountable, and for this reason, until the 90s, the Forex was still considered a market reserved only for a select few, in particular to the banks and to subjects with great financial resources.

The technology, however, has proved once again fundamental for the evolution of Forex, as the advent of the internet has allowed the opening of the trading world also to aspiring traders and investors with limited financial resources. The costs, in fact, have been gradually reduced and trading has increasingly become an open market.

1.2 – The main advantages

The Forex market allows trading on international transactions, with the possibility of obtaining many gains. Many individuals have managed to make Forex trading a real job, but what really distinguishes the Forex from any other market are the advantages connected to the activity carried out.

The main advantage is the low commission costs. Online trading has indeed made it possible to reduce this burden which for years had characterized the financial market. The commissions present today in

Forex are relative to the broker that you choose to use to carry out your business, but they are in any case minimal.

Another advantage regards the full autonomy possessed by the trader. The decision to open a position, to close it, to trade first-hand or to rely on automated systems is entirely up to every investor. In modern trading, the figure of the intermediary is almost completely gone, thanks to the possibility of acting through simple clicks directly on the market. This is possible because Forex has a very high market liquidity, which allows traders to remain active in trading at any time, buying and selling positions in the market.

Another advantageous consequence of the advent of technology in financial markets and in particular in Forex is the possibility to carry out trading at any time of day or night, for five days a week, excluding the weekend during which all financial markets in the world are closed.

Modern trading allows traders to make their own investments, allocating small amounts for each individual transaction. This is possible thanks to the financial leverage tool made available by the brokers, which allows positions to be opened with values significantly higher than the sum invested.

The advent of smartphones and tablets has allowed traders to also expand the concept of trading. The operations can be managed easily from anywhere, with the only requirement being that of having a stable internet connection. In this way, both the chances of exploiting price changes in real-time and, consequently, profits grow. Therefore, it is no longer necessary for the trader to physically go to the bank or, in general, to the financial institution to carry out his transaction.

The sudden increase in the number of aspiring traders, who face the world of Forex often without a sufficient statistical and financial basis, has led brokers to create free demos that allow them to simulate trading activity using a virtual monetary balance, thus eliminating the risks and at the same time allowing them to improve their affinity with the proposed interface.

Finally, trading is often mistakenly seen as an insecure activity. In reality, everything that takes place within the Forex market is constantly monitored and verified by supervisory and control bodies.

Each broker can obtain different certifications, to guarantee the quality of the service offered and the honesty of the activity. This can be translated as total security in the investment that it will make.

1.3 – The subjects in the Forex market

In order to fully understand the Forex, it is essential to know who the subjects are, who in a more or less active way, participate in the movement of prices and in the definition of the meeting point between supply and demand. For many years, the largest financial market in the world has only been opened to a few investors who have certain economic requirements.

Fortunately, the web has marked the definitive opening of Forex to all previously excluded subjects, regardless of the purpose for which they have decided to appear in this market or the way in which they invest. Generally, the subjects decide to carry out trading only for speculative purposes, but a small slice of the active subjects participates in the Forex with the purpose of converting money in currencies different from the one possessed.

The main subjects of Forex are the Merchant Banks, known more simply as business banks. These subjects perform different functions: firstly, being credit institutions, they perform a service related to financial advisory activity and, secondly, they manage assets, sometimes considerable, of private subjects. By not performing commercial functions, it is not possible for private citizens to deposit funds with Merchant Banks. Experts consider these subjects to be the fundamental part of the entire Forex market because, by exploiting their interests, they allow the movement of around 50% of the entire volume of exchanges.

But the Merchant Banks are not the only banking institutions present within Forex. Central Banks are in fact fundamental, which administer national monetary policy, and based on the decisions taken, influence the interest rates present in the Forex market. But the hypothetical power of the central banks is even higher than this. In fact, they periodically make forecasts about future market trends and based on these estimates, traders will make their investments. So this is an indirect but still decisive influence.

There are also institutions that allow traders to bring together the individual capitals in a single investment fund, in order to carry out a single trading activity and to share the profits obtained among the same traders on the basis of the shares assigned. These institutions are called mutual funds.

Instead of the latter, the Hedge Funds, which act within the Forex trying to exploit transactions with a maturity in the very short term, allocating huge investments. Profits are guaranteed, in the case of a positive transaction, thanks to the effect of financial leverage, which is very high in this type of investment. However, in order to access these types of funds, in addition to a high level of economic availability, a series of requirements that limit participation is also required.

The Forex market is also open to multinationals, which exploit the potential of the market to buy certain products or financial instruments in a given currency, to resell them immediately, or at the right time, to another currency. Their purpose is therefore not speculative, but rather that of reducing exchange costs.

Traders represent the last category of subjects that are activated within the Forex market. Of course, whether they are professional investors or not, they act for pure personal profit. Private traders do not enjoy great advantages, which are reserved especially for other subjects. In fact, they cannot get news in advance relating to certain transactions and cannot enjoy reduced spreads.

There are, however, two further categories of subjects that are often heard mentioning within the Forex market, namely bears and bulls. These two animals symbolically represent those who voluntarily influence the market trend. Bulls are those who would like a bull market to make the most of their entry into the Forex with long-term operations. The bears, on the other hand, are more simply the active sellers of Forex, which therefore tend to a bear market to make profits from the trading operations carried out. The market, therefore, fluctuates depending on the strength of these two categories, which continually push the trend up or down. Naturally, a domain of the bulls would translate into a positive trend, with the points of maximum and minimum reaching ever-higher levels, while domination of the bears would lead to a symmetrically opposite situation. For traders, it is convenient that one of the two forces prevails over the other since in case of equilibrium we would find ourselves in one of the lateral phases of the market, during which making profits would prove complex. The names given to active buyers and sellers of Forex are derived from the way in which these two animals attack. The bull tends to enchant the challenger with a movement that goes from the bottom upwards, while the bear tends to attack the preys using the legs, therefore with a movement that goes from top to bottom.

The general opinion that is created by combining the opinions of every single active subject present in the Forex takes the name of market sentiment. Therefore, traders will have to study and investigate what the dominant attitude in the market at that precise moment is, so as to guess what the future trend of the trend may be.

1.4 – Capital management

Trading is an activity in which it is necessary to contemplate risk. This means that opening positions can both bring net profits in the medium-long term, and lead to huge losses affecting the allocated capital. To avoid squandering the entire capital, it is therefore essential to implement a strategy aimed at the management of capital, which is called Money Management. The objective of this analysis is certainly to bring the trader to optimize profits and minimize losses. These cannot be eliminated, as they are inherent in the concept of trading itself, but must be controlled and contained. There are no perfect capital management strategies, and each theory has strengths and weaknesses. However, almost all of them are based on the same key points, to be taken as real Forex dogmas. The lack of a Money Management or in any case the adoption of an unsuitable and little-studied strategy will certainly push the trader to failure.

It is possible to break down the capital management strategy into two components, which can be analyzed separately but which in reality are inseparable from each other. The first component is Risk Management, which consists of analyzing and studying each position that you intend to open in the Forex. The second component is the Position Sizing, which aims to identify what is the optimal amount of capital to be allocated for each transaction to be performed in trading.

Money Management is also risk management. It is necessary to know that the profits necessary to return to the initial capital in case of loss are proportional to the loss.

One of the most important concepts of Money Management and the whole Forex is that of drawdown. This element is nothing more than the reduction of capital due to a series of negative transactions and indicates, in percentage terms, the risk present in the open position. It is essential not to underestimate the drawdown as this establishes what the limit is, based on the allocated capital and the amount of losses, beyond which it becomes impossible to continue trading. An adequate strategy of Money Management tends to define what this limit is, so as to be kept as far as possible from it. As mentioned, although varies, all Money Management strategies are based on some essential aspects. First of all, each trader must have an amount of initial capital that is suitable for trading. Starting in a state of undercapitalization can induce the trader, following an initial series of negative transactions to immediately exit the Forex. At the same time, it is necessary to define what the usable allocated capital limit is. Experts generally advise not to exceed two-thirds of the total capital. Also, for this reason, it is important to intelligently program the operations to be performed. Opening multiple locations at the same time can be beneficial, but also very dangerous. Also, in this case, the advice is to never invest more than 20% of the capital at the same time.

It is important to keep in mind what the objectives of each operation are. The trading must be carried out already determining in advance a maximum limit of loss, which is called stop loss, and a considered optimal level of profit, that is the take profit. Once the trend goes beyond one of the two points, for different reasons, it is recommended to close the position. The reason is to take into consideration a ratio between yield and risk neither too high nor too low. It is sometimes risky and counterproductive to try to let a profit go too far, especially if the take profit point has already been passed. The trend could change orientation and start producing loss, squandering the gain made. For this reason, it is sometimes important to anticipate the closure of a positive transaction in order to make a profit anyway.

A correct application of its capital management strategy will allow traders to remain on the Forex in the long run, even during the negative phases of trading. If the negative operations seem to have no end, the strategy created is not the right one for the Forex and therefore it will be necessary to re-determine the fundamental principles of Money Management.

1.5 – Forex Trading Indices

The number of trades traded within Forex in a given period represents the volume of market trades. This figure is one of the most important indicators to analyze by traders before entering the Forex market and being decisive in choosing whether or not to open a position.

The volume of trade varies depending on the price trend. Markets with low trading volumes are easily identifiable graphically. They have a substantial equivalence of the level of the prices assumed at the time of opening with the prices of the moment of closure. In addition, the bars or candles that make up the graph are very small. The main feature of the markets with high trading volumes is the considerable distance between maximums and minimums, with very long bars or candles.

Another indicator is called the Percentage in Point, known more simply with the acronym PIP. The Percentage in Point is the change in price suffered by a given currency, however it may be small. Therefore, this instrument is fundamental to verify what the effective variation is, but also allows to establish what the gains and losses are. However, the calculation of the

PIP is very simple. In fact, observing the value assumed by the price at two different times, the PIP corresponds to the difference between the fourth decimal digit of the two values.

As previously stated, the trading market was profoundly different in the past. In fact, in order to invest in Forex, brokers required very high access costs and commissions to possess a sort of selection and control function on the activity carried out by traders. The internet has also allowed other subjects to become Forex brokers and this has led to a natural reduction in market access prices. This was possible thanks to financial leverage, which allowed traders to trade in the Forex lots by taking money in the form of a loan directly from the broker chosen to trade.

The leverage is expressed in the form of a proportion, in which the first number represents the maximum movable value, while the second number is the reference of the invested value. Therefore, in a proportion of 400: 1 for every Euro invested, it is possible to handle a maximum amount of 400 Euro. Of course, the expansion allowed on leverage from financial leverage is also reflected in the losses.

Therefore, both the yield and the risk increase with this tool. For this reason, if trading is done using financial leverage, it becomes fundamental to establish the stop loss and take profit points with great rationality, which will guarantee a balance to the investment.

1.6 – The times at which to trade

One of the characteristics that push traders to invest in the Forex market is the possibility of being able to invest at any time, for five days a week. Specifically, the Forex opens at 11.00 pm on Sunday, taking into consideration the Italian timetable, and closes at the same time on Friday. There are times that allow traders to make more profits and those during which there is both a high volume of trades and a high rate of volatility. Indeed, the combination of these two factors guarantees a much more evident trend, but at the same time, the high volatility induces an increase in the risk rate, caused by the high unpredictability inherent in the movement made by prices. During the opening hours, however, Forex also presents moments in which the volatility and the volume of trade take on values so low that it seems unnecessary to invest or open positions. These are the moments that follow the opening of the market on Sunday, and those that precede Friday closing.

However, it is possible to distinguish three different sessions, which alternate during the day.

1.6.1 – Forex in America

The opening time of the Forex for what concerns the American session is at 14:00 Italian time, while the closing time is 23:00. The American market makes it possible to handle a very high volume of trade. Furthermore, the overlapping and simultaneous trading between the American session and the European session guarantee a favorable situation. During this session, traders must essentially consider two times: the first is 18:00, the second is 20:00, again based on Italian time. In fact, at these times every day, the FED or the US central bank makes announcements that could upset the trends. Therefore the advice is to carry out trading operations only on the US dollar and on the Canadian one once the time of the first announcement made by the Federal Reserve System has been exceeded.

1.6.2 – Forex in Europa

The session in Europe opens at 8:00 am Italian time to close when the FED makes its first announcement, that is, at 6.00 pm. The main feature of this market is the presence of decisive and important movements, which take place mainly starting at 9:00. In fact, starting from this time, news about the variations in the exchange rate of the currencies begin to reach the markets, modifying the trend of the present trends. In this market, the greatest advantages are provided by the transactions carried out on the trading relating to the Euro and those relating to the Swiss Franc.

1.6.3 – Forex in Asia

The Asian session has times that do not coincide with those of the American session and those of the European session. The Forex in Asia opens at the closing time of the American Forex, that is at 23:00 and closes at the opening time of theEuropean Forex, that is at 8:00. It is perhaps the session that moves fewer trade volumes but has large squares that are fundamental for the entire Forex market, such as those in Tokyo and Hong Kong. Having a schedule of activities that is not very influential at a global level from a macroeconomic and financial point of view, the trend seems to take on a linear trend, which does not present excessive fluctuations or real shocks, unless there are really sensational events.

Chapter 2 - Orders in Forex Trading

In the world of online Forex trading, it is possible to make a consistent variety of orders, selecting the instruments with which you want to trade and studying trends in the various markets in real-time through the use of graphical charts. To operate in such markets, it is necessary to have knowledge of the various orders that can be made in the various trading platforms to give the broker precise indications that allow obtaining positive results.

The main types are stop losses, take profits, market orders, and limit orders.

2.1 – Stop-loss

Stop-loss orders are a fundamental tool for traders to manage Forex-related risk, thanks to which it is possible to limit the losses that can arise from a negative phase of the market. For this reason, it is a protection order, through which the maximum value of the loss of capital that the trader is willing to tolerate for a single open position will be set. This order must be set by the trader in advance with respect to the execution of the various opening transactions and will be executed completely automatically by the Forex platform used. When the trend reaches the fixed stop-loss level, the position will be automatically closed to prevent losses from reaching a level that will irreparably erode the capital.

To set the stop-loss point, it is necessary to monitor the volatility of the main currency pairs. If the order is of minor importance, small losses may occur, vice versa, for orders of greater importance, the losses could compromise the totality of the profits of the trader.

Through the stop-loss, it is possible to safeguard the investments from sudden changes in the market, determining the maximum loss achievable based on one's own Forex trading strategy, managing the risk in the most appropriate way.

The greatest losses occur when the trade is closed and the stop-loss order is executed at a time when the market is going through a phase of changes that could generate profits instead. In this case, it is possible to set the strategy in such a way that additional positions are opened to recover the losses previously incurred. However, even this system can prove to be a failure, as the market often suffers from sudden changes, due to the diffusion of important financial news, which is unable to make profits, but leads to further losses.

The stop-loss order is the basis for building an efficient trading strategy. For this reason, three systems of stop values will be generated based on the volatility of the trade: a system with a high stop for cases of high volatility, a system with a low stop for cases of low volatility, an intermediate system. Automatic trading systems analyze the signals to assess the level at which to set the stop-loss.

Traders do not always adhere to established stop-loss orders but continue to keep positions at a loss in the hope that the trend will change its trend and turn losses into profits. However, this interference with the implemented strategy will only generate larger losses, putting the entire capital at risk.

2.2 – Take Profit

The second type of fundamental orders for the management of Forex trading operations is take profit. It stands in contrast to the stop-loss and indicates the level of protection of profits. Like the stop-loss, it must be set before executing market transactions, based on the trader's strategy and financial availability. In a sense, it is a limit to earnings, which is activated once the previously established levels are reached, to prevent market changes from eroding these gains and nullifying what has been done up to that point.

What takes the take profit is a purely prudential function. At the same time, a trader can doubt that the trade, once it has gone beyond the take profit level, can continue in its positive trend and the closure of the early position could prove to be a missed opportunity. But the task of take profit can also be understood as a limit to the trader's greed, which could lead to higher earnings, but also very large losses. Human emotion is a characteristic that in the world of Forex should be completely zeroed. Greed naturally falls within the feelings to be eliminated, and letting go of profit means facing a risk that becomes higher every second. However, choosing the exact point in which to place the take profit is not easy. The choice may depend essentially on the motivation that pushes the trader to make a certain investment, which can be mainly attributed to two cases: the first involves the identification of a specific graphic figure that the trend is going to complete; the second relates to the pursuit of the trend undertaken by the trend. If the trader has identified a partial figure by analyzing the graph of the price fluctuation, investing on the conclusion of the trend, the take profit must be fixed at the point where it is assumed that the representation that led to the opening of the position will be concluded. The decision of where to fix the take profit in the event that the trader opens the position in order to follow a specific trend is instead subordinated to the levels of support and resistance. These represent fundamental points since it is assumed that in the areas in which the same are present, the trend can reverse its trend. Of course, in the event that the investment refers to a purchase transaction, the take profit must be positioned below the resistance level; vice versa, in a sales transaction, the take profit will have to be set a few points above the support level.

2.3 – Market orders

Market orders must be conceived as communications that each trader sends to their broker: the communication involves the willingness to buy at the selling price present at a given time or to sell at the demand price present at the time the transaction is opened.

For simplification, in market orders, the offer price is indicated with the abbreviation ASK, while the demand price with the abbreviation BID; the difference between the two price values is known as SPREAD.

The market order does not require any requirement to be executed, except the will of the trader, and its opening is immediate. However, it is possible to distinguish two different types of market orders, first type is called long orders, and the second type is called short orders.

The first type refers to purchase orders that the trader decides to execute when he or she is convinced that the price of the instrument observed may experience a rise in subsequent periods.

The second type represents a category of orders attributable to short selling. These types of orders are executed by the trader when he or she assumes that the trend can move downwards in a very short term.

2.4 – Limit orders

If the market orders do not require any particular requirement for their execution, the limit orders require the occurrence of a specific event in order to be executed. The trading platform used will place the investment immediately, but the same will be executed only if the price trend exceeds the limit that the trader has previously set. It is possible to execute four different types of limit orders.

The first type is called Buy Limit, and it is an order that is used if the trader expects the price trend to continue the downward trend. However, the operation will be performed by opening a buying position when the trend exceeds a certain limit, thus anticipating the trend reversal. To carry out an order of this kind, the condition must be set at a lower price than the one present at the time of the investment.

A second category is the Buy Stop order. The trader, in this case, expects a continuation of the price trend but will open a long position only after the trend has reached a certain limit. In this case, the level of the limit must be set at a higher point than the value possessed by the price at the time the position is opened.

Sell Limit orders, on the other hand, are used if the trader intends to open a short position, but before opening the position, he or she wants to make sure that the downward trend reaches a certain level. Also, in this case, the requirement that determines the effective realization of the trading is the achievement of a condition set at a lower value than the one possessed by the price at the time of the order.

Finally, the last type of orders is represented by Sell Stop orders. The trader expects the price to continue its upward trend but once a certain limit is reached, it reverses its performance. Therefore the point at which the Sell Stop is set must be at a higher level than the price at the time the order is placed.

Chapter 3 - Fundamental Analysis and Technical Analysis

In the world of Forex, the study of all the macroeconomic events that are able to manipulate, or at least influence the price trend and the entire market trend is very important. This type of analysis is called macroeconomic analysis, but it is known to all traders as Fundamental Analysis. The purpose of the Fundamental Analysis is to identify the economic news related to a specific country and try to understand how the announcements of such news affect the value of the currency traded in that country. However, the Fundamental Analysis refers to an economic calendar, containing all the events, identified both according to a chronological criterion and according to a national criterion, which could influence the level of the various currencies. The web now abounds with economic calendars, more or less detailed, and for traders it is easier to identify and wait for economic news. The most complete economic calendars make it possible to relate the data relating to an economic event with those present on the same day in previous years, but also with those expected for the current year, so as to provide traders with a clear and complete overview based on which it is possible to carry out an in-depth study of Fundamental Analysis. The tools needed to carry out a correct fundamental analysis are the macroeconomic indicators. Being aware of the presence or otherwise of certain economic news is the first step that every trader, professional or not, must take before trading.

If Fundamental Analysis studies the economic news and their impact on the world of Forex, the Technical Analysis, through a detailed analysis relating to the trend of prices within the market, aims to define what their behavior could be in a more or less distant future. To do this, the Technical Analysis relies on various statistical tools, but also tends to evaluate the human behaviors that, according to this theory, influence trend oscillations more than anything else. The Technical Analysis has its primary purpose of identifying and analyzing all the possible levels of entry and exit from the market in such a way that the trader can choose the best entry, thanks to certain tools increasingly advanced from the technological point of view. There are essentially two instruments on which the

Technical Analysis is based: first of all the technical indicators, which on the basis of the statistical data in possession, provide interesting information regarding the price trend; secondly, the graphic tools, which work more on the visual part to offer the trader a clear image of the market trend. Of course, both tools require analysis software capable of transposing data and externalizing it in the best possible way so that it can be understood by the trader. These softwares are readily available on the web: sometimes, however, the work done is not sufficiently clear and detailed, in particular if it is a matter of software downloaded for free from the Internet.

3.1 – Fundamental Analysis: macroeconomic indicators

As previously stated, Fundamental Analysis bases its effectiveness on some macroeconomic indicators.

The first of these indicators is certainly the national Gross Domestic Product, also known with the acronym PIL. This indicator is given by the sum of all the goods and services that are produced within the national boundaries in a given period of time, to then be consumed. The Gross Domestic Product greatly influences the Forex, as a possible announcement of its increase involves a positive phase, vice versa its reduction is closely related to a market contraction.

A second macroeconomic indicator which is very important for Fundamental Analysis is the data relating to industrial production. This figure, not considering the building sector, indicates what production refers to the industrial sector of a given country only. Also in this case, as for GDP, industrial production and Forex are proportional and the increase in the former determines an expansive phase of the latter, while a decline would cause a negative phase.

Fundamental Analysis can also rely on an indicator that aims to exclude all indirect sales, including services, from GDP and is called a retail sales index. Also for this macroeconomic indicator, the relationship with Forex is strictly proportional.

The indicator relating to durable goods orders refers to the volume expressed in the national currency of durable goods, that is, those goods that offer their utility over several years, such as cars, which have been produced by the manufacturing sector of a nation. The market strengthens when this indicator increases and weakens when the indicator decreases.

Interest rates are also among the indispensable macroeconomic indicators for Fundamental Analysis, as they affect both the monetary policy implemented by central banks and the economic choices of a country. In this case, the effects caused by an increase in interest rates are double: initially an increase is obtained in the volatility rate present in the Forex. Subsequently, this translates into an expansion of the market. Conversely, a reduction in the rate causes a weakening of the market.

Through the relationship between the incidence of the employed population and the total population of a given country, it is possible to know the national employment indicator. Positive values of this indicator determine favorable market phases, on the contrary, negative values lead to phases of decline.

The difference between exports and imports, that is the national trade balance, determines the last of the main macroeconomic indicators that influence the Forex market.

3.2 – The three pillars of Technical Analysis

As mentioned above, the Technical Analysis is aimed at forecasting the trend of financial markets, to allow those who intend to carry out investment transactions to be able to make profits with greater probability. This analysis is very complex and is based on three basic assumptions: prices discount everything, the market moves by trends and history repeats itself.

The first assumption indicates that the prices on the market reflect all the economic information available, even those known only to a few subjects. Therefore, it is not necessary to research and analyze this information, as it is already contained in price fluctuations.

The second assumption indicates that price fluctuations are never random, but the result of the combination of two or more trends. The Technical Analysis aims to identify these trends and predict their evolution over time. Therefore the trader in the context of this analysis will not have to pretend to sell at the maximum price levels or to buy at the minimum levels but will have to exploit the trend in place at that time.

The third prerequisite indicates the cyclical nature of the financial market trend. This aspect is mainly due to the willingness of human beings to make profits from trading, which leads them to periodically repeat the same behaviors, sometimes even in a frenetic way. It is therefore important to analyze the time series, which tend to identify price patterns useful for understanding what the trend of the trend may be in the future.

The assumptions of the Technical Analysis do not guarantee the infallibility of the forecasts but aim to formulate forecasts with a percentage of correctness equal to at least 70%, to be able to extricate even the most hostile financial markets.

3.3 – Dow's Theory

The Modern Technical Analysis is the result of a series of studies carried out by an American, Charles Dow, a journalist who in the early twentieth century published a series of theories concerning the analysis of financial markets in the Wall Street Journal. These theories have been used as a basis for the study and examination of further doctrines, because of the effectiveness and adaptability shown also for the systems present in modern markets.

Dow's theory is based on the idea that price fluctuations do not depend on purely random factors, but that these depend on certain trends, more or less predictable. These oscillations are also compared by the journalist to the waves of the sea, which periodically advance and retract, depending on the tides. Only when the trends come to almost completely exhaust their strength, then will there be a reversal of the trend and the cyclicality will resume from the beginning.

Dow, in order to organize his theory, set six fundamental points of his analysis.

The first assumption of Dow's theory also coincides with one of the basic principles of

Technical Analysis, namely that according to which prices discount everything. So according to Dow, the price contains in itself all the information, even those that are difficult to find, and it is sufficient to analyze it to become aware of the economic events that have characterized it.

The second point of Dow's Theory identifies three different possible trends that can be assumed by the price within the financial market, which differ only in duration. The first type is called as the primary trend, which has a significantly longer duration than the other two categories, as it can follow its trend fluctuation even for periods longer than one year. The second type is called the secondary trend, which has a variable duration between ninety and one hundred and eighty days. Finally, the last type is called the minor trend, which generally lasts less than a month and is not always easily identifiable on the market.

In the third point, Dow proceeds in his theory by breaking down every single type of trend into three further categories, which are called phases, so as to facilitate understanding of the market and identifying the motivations that drive prices towards recruitment of a certain trend. The first of the three phases is defined by Dow as an

Accumulation phase, and it is fundamental because during this interval, the trend begins to take shape. However, only a few traders will be able to get to know the economic information and fully exploit this awareness. The trend is still in one of its lateral phases and shows no intention of varying its oscillation. Therefore, it is impossible to graphically recognize that it is in an accumulation phase. The second phase, known as the Participation phase, shows the first signs that can be distinguished also graphically from the formation of a new trend, as we are witnessing an initial price increase. The increasingly consistent entry into the market of traders, even those not informed, pushes the price level ever higher until this influence diminishes causing the trend to slow. It is certainly the phase of the trend most favorable for investors, during which the market presents very high trading volumes and a level of volatility. The third phase, finally, is defined by Dow as a Distribution phase and represents the time interval during which the price has reached its maximum and investors intuit that it is the opportune moment to close the open positions in the Forex, decreeing the trend reversal. It is a very hectic phase because the traders have entered a state similar to panic, to be able to sell the position at the best possible price, and start a frantic race to the bottom.

Analyzing the rail and US industrial index, Dow was able to identify a direct correlation between the two, an event that allowed him to establish the fourth point of his theory. According to Dow, these two indexes have an indissoluble positive link that makes it unable to confirm a trend reversal if this situation is observed only in one of the two. This concept can also be applied to the currencies of various countries in the Forex market.

The fifth point envisages another method of identifying the trend, which is derived, according to Dow, from the observation of the trading volumes present within the market. They are sometimes even able to anticipate the trend, but they must be analyzed above all in order to confirm it. In fact, each trend is associated with a significant increase in volumes, while the lateral phases present substantial reductions in them. This means that it is possible to confirm that there is a trend only after verifying the expansion of the volumes..

The sixth point in Dow's Theory is perhaps the most complicated. He states that every trend must be considered as such until a clear sign of the inversion appears in the graph. Until then, especially for those who adopt a Trend Following strategy, it is necessary to follow the trend. Clearly, it is complicated to anticipate the reversal of the trend, especially when there is a price drop due to a financial correction.

3.4 – The Momentum and Fibonacci retracements

Once the trend has been identified, each investor, in order to increase the probability of success, must analyze both the structure and the intensity. In particular this last feature, known in the Forex also as Momentum, gives the opportunity to understand if the trend can last a long time or if it is running out of its strength, turning towards a lateral market phase. Furthermore, finding out which is the Momentum offers traders the chance to guess, through the analysis called market divergences, when the end of the trend will occur.

The concept of Momentum has deep ties with physics and in particular with Newton's three laws. It is necessary to imagine that prices are like bodies, while the subjects that influence Forex are forces: both components respond to the laws of dynamics composed by the English mathematician.

Following this logic, the prices and the active subjects of the market can become the protagonists of the three laws of dynamics. According to the first law, prices are subject to fluctuations according to the announced economic news, and always on the basis of it, the subjects will enter the market. For the second law, the thrust and intensity of the trend will be proportional to the number of subjects who decide to purchase the positions. Finally, according to the third law, once the maximum point is reached, the price trend will undergo a push of equal magnitude, completely opposite, which will lead to a trend reversal.

The correlation between physics and financial markets helps to understand what the importance of momentum is. It, in fact, intended as a variation of the intensity of the trend in a given time interval, undergoes increases when the price trend is subject to important accelerations: a high momentum indicates that the trend will continue in the trend direction.

The momentum assumes high values only on three occasions: firstly, when the trend is forming, or when there is a trend reversal and finally during the lateral market phases. Studying the momentum allows us to guess what the future price trend may be, helping the trader to accumulate profits.

Currently, it is possible to identify the momentum through the use of some indicators, among which we recall the moving averages, the Bollinger bands, the RSI, the ADX and the stochastic oscillator.

In order to identify the possible levels that the price can take in the immediate future, many traders decide to use the Fibonacci retracements. The latter was an Italian mathematician who lived in 1200, who had identified a sort of proportion between any two elements, even those found in nature, which have different sizes. Fibonacci, based on a hypothetical golden section, identifies a sequence of numbers, in which each digit is given by the sum of the last two numbers preceding it. This sequence has been successfully applied also in the world of trading and is now a very important tool that traders use to analyze the market.

The purpose of Fibonacci retracements is to identify some points, which no other instrument is able to detect, which could become supports or resistances. In this way, the trader is able to anticipate a trend reversal, obtaining considerable advantages.

3.5 – Overbought and oversold

In Forex there are situations in which prices reach certain levels, located in particular areas of the market.

In particular, the overbought zone refers to an area in which the price trend is found which has suffered an excessive rise. So once the trend has reached this area, the traders expect that there will be a reversal of the trend that brings prices back into a standard range. The prices reach these areas on extraordinary occasions and remain there for a relatively short time. The excessive rise is caused by the struggle between bulls and bears that characterizes the financial market. Initially, the excessive rise caused the bulls, that is the buyers, to close the open positions on the market in order to make profits. At the same time, bears, or sellers, have taken advantage of the situation by selling in the open. All this is reflected graphically with an initial surge of the trend towards the overbought area and a subsequent dive for a return to normality.

Symmetrically, the oversold areas identify those downgraded areas where prices have gone, exceeding the minimum periodic limits. In this case, the traders expect a surge that brings the trend back to the standard average of the period. Even the reasons are opposite to those that create surges in the overbought areas. In this case, the bears, due to the excessively low price, decided to close their positions, while the bulls hypothesized that the trend could soon be traced, opening positions. These actions first sank the trend beyond the periodic minimum, and then returned it to its standard range.

Chapter 4 - Indicators and oscillators

In order to analyze Forex more thoroughly, a series of indicators or oscillators have been made available to traders. These are intended to confirm or deny the credibility of each individual signal received. There is nothing certain in the world of trading. Therefore, it is wrong to think that indicators and oscillators can somehow predict the future, indicating with certainty the values that the prices will assume. They must be thought of as support tools, which increase the chances of earning, but which are certainly not infallible.

4.1 – The moving averages

Moving averages are the most used indicator by investors in Forex and other financial markets. Thanks to this type of indicator, it is possible to outline the tendency that the market will take on, but also to generate some signals so that the trader can promptly open or close a certain position. Moving averages can be divided into three sub-categories: the simple moving average, the weighted one and the exponential one. These differ from each other depending on the calculation method, giving greater weight to the events of the past that are more distant, as is the case for the exponential moving average, or more recent, as is the case for the weighted moving average.

The use of moving averages makes it possible to identify the primary trend, reducing all those corrections that distort the attention of the trader and which cause valuation errors during the trading activity.

4.2 - Bollinger bands

Through the Bollinger bands the trader can identify the volatility present in the market and report it directly on the chart. This indicator is composed of three lines: the upper band, the lower band, and the balance line. The first band moves above the price line, the second below it, while the third follows the moving average of price values. This indicator has many functions. First of all, it is used to identify the volatility present in the market: the bands widen when the volatility is high and shrink when the volatility takes on low values. Furthermore, the Bollinger bands are used to confirm the intensity of a given trend and to identify the overbought and oversold areas. Finally, this oscillator makes it possible to determine the areas in which supports and resistances are present.

This tool can be very useful especially if used in combination with other indicators, to evaluate, and eventually confirm, the meaning of market signals.

4.3 – Relative Strenght Index

The Relative Strength Index, better known with the acronym RSI, is an indicator of fundamental importance for the execution of trading as it helps to evaluate the correct speed with which prices change. It is one of the most used indicators that, although difficult to understand, is inserted by the brokers directly into the platforms so that traders can use it without difficulty.

The RSI makes it possible to understand the area to which the price belongs at a particular moment and, in particular, identifies the overbought and oversold areas, thus allowing investors to open the positions correctly.

Generally, the range in which the Relative Strength Index moves is between the value 0 and the value 100. This allows us to always have objective data, regardless of the observed trend. This indicator takes specific values to indicate that the trend is in particular areas and specifically: the RSI is above 70 if the price is in an overbought zone, and is less than 30 if the price is found in an oversold area.

4.4 – Adverage Directional Index

Through the Adverage Directional Index, it is possible to understand what the actual strength or intensity of a trend is. This indicator, also known by the acronym ADX, is graphically represented by a line that oscillates between 0 and 100: the trend appears strong if the ADX takes values greater than 40, while it is considered congested when it takes values below 20.

Therefore, using this indicator, it is not possible to understand if the trend is in a rising or falling phase, but only if one is or is not in a trend phase.

The ADX consists of three lines: the Line + DI, calculated on the basis of the difference between the maximum of the current day and that of the previous day; the Line −DI, calculated on the basis of the difference between the minimum of the current day and that of the previous day; the ADX Line, which is based on the relationship between the two previous lines.

Based on the values assumed by these three lines, the trader can guess whether the market is in a trend phase or not.

4.5 – The stochastic oscillator

If the trader intends to identify which time intervals are characterized by accumulation or by price distribution, then it is necessary to use the stochastic oscillator. This is one of the most powerful tools of the entire market analysis, able to understand what the probable future price trend is. The stochastic oscillator examines the position taken by the closing prices: if these are approaching the maximum daily levels, then the trend will probably be on the upside, while if they approach the daily minimums the trend will tend to fall. Also, in this case, the range assumes values that oscillate between the value 0 and the value 100.

The analysis of the stochastic oscillator is based on two elements. First of all, the Curve% K, which relates the closing prices in a given interval, and secondly the Curve% D, which instead operates on the levels assumed by the first curve. In this case, the overbought areas are identified when the oscillator takes values greater than 80, while those of oversold are assumed to have values below 20.

In short, with the stochastic user, it is possible to identify, in addition to the overbought and oversold areas, also the areas that anticipate trend reversals. It also sends the trader signals for opening or closing the position, based on the data obtained by crossing the% K and% D curves.

Conclusions

The analysis carried out in this guide has shown that Forex can be a winning bet, especially if done in a professional manner.

Of course, the risk of suffering losses cannot be eliminated completely, but by implementing an efficient strategy, through the study and analysis of the various indicators, it will be possible to reduce the incidence and protect the capital invested.

Being aware of the risk is the first fundamental step to increase the chances of achieving positive results in the Forex market. Thanks to this sort of limit it will be possible to avoid suffering serious losses and at the same time obtaining reasonable profits.

www.ingramcontent.com/pod-product-compliance
Lightning Source LLC
Chambersburg PA
CBHW060822220526
45466CB00003B/945